Sensational
Sugar Fairies

Dedication

To my sister Annie and my friend Anne for their
continued love, support and advice.

Sensational
Sugar Fairies

FRANCES MCNAUGHTON

Search Press

Acknowledgements

Thanks to all at Search Press, especially Roz, Sophie, Marrianne and Paul for their help in this project.

Special thanks to Rainbow Dust Colours, Patchwork Cutters, FPC Sugarcraft Moulds and Ellen's Creative Cakes.

First published in Great Britain 2013

Search Press Limited
Wellwood, North Farm Road,
Tunbridge Wells, Kent TN2 3DR

Illustrations and text copyright ©
Frances McNaughton 2013

Photographs by Paul Bricknell at
Search Press Studio

Photographs and design copyright
© Search Press Ltd. 2013

Printed in China

ISBN: 978-1-84448-865-0

Suppliers
If you have difficulty in obtaining any of the materials and equipment mentioned in this book, then please visit the Search Press website for details of suppliers:
www.searchpress.com

You are invited to visit the author's website:
franklysweet.co.uk

Contents

Introduction

When I was a little girl, I loved fairies and fairy stories. I still have a fascination for fantasy and a love of the 'little people'. I have a friend who, when her granddaughters were young, used to help the fairies write messages to them in miniature envelopes containing petals, glitter or other tiny items from the garden. She would tuck these into an old tree in her garden for the children to find. The girls would delight in writing back to the fairies with their news, put their letters back in the tree, and eagerly await the next visit to their grandmother to see if the fairies had replied. This beautiful fantasy continued for years until the girls grew up and found other interests, and the fairies had to turn their attention to other children.

I created my first sugar fairy book ten years ago, and have the pleasure of knowing that many new fairies have been made following its instructions, and also in the many classes I have taught over the years. It has been a real delight to see the fairies emerging at workshops; some of them beautiful, some perhaps a little 'challenged' in the legs or faces! As in real life, all are special in their own way!

When modelling the fairies for this new book, I wanted to keep the projects as simple as I could so that people can gain inspiration and make the fairies themselves. For this reason I have used small head moulds, as it is so important to feel that you can accomplish making a beautiful fairy. Some of you may already be able to model tiny faces without the use of moulds. I take you step-by-step through all the stages of making each figure: painting different faces; shaping bodies and limbs by hand; designing hairstyles; creating beautiful outfits; making wings in various ways; and using colouring methods such as mixing, dusting and painting for different effects. In this way you will learn many techniques which can be used to make figures of your own design, including non-fairy models. Inspiration for the fairies has come from many different places, and I tell you more about this at the beginning of each project.

One of the joys in my life has been teaching people the skills I have learned over the years, and in many cases these people have gone on to teach sugarcraft to others. Teaching sugarcraft has taken me to different countries, and has given me the chance to meet and teach a lot of lovely people. It has also given me great pleasure to make these beautiful creations, although these days there never seems to be time to 'play'! There is a lot of pleasure and pride in making delicious cakes for special occasions and decorating them with something beautiful you have made.

I hope you will enjoy this book, and that the fairies will grant your wishes and bring you happiness.

Safe in the tree top, this baby fairy sleeps soundly in a re-used bird's nest. The tree was made by attaching long thin sausages of sugarpaste to the dampened cake, forming the trunk and branching out at the top. The trunk and branches were textured with a Dresden tool and knife, then painted with different shades of dark brown. Fine branches and simple leaves were painted directly on to the cake. Finally a few small cut-out sugarpaste leaves were stuck in place to give the appearance of a tree in spring.

Materials

Modelling materials

Mexican paste

This is a sugar modelling paste made with gum, which makes it stronger and allows it to be rolled out thinly for the clothes. I have used it to make the bodies of the fairies. It dries slowly, which is useful when positioning limbs. It is available commercially or can be made using the following recipe:

Place 227g (8oz) icing sugar (confectioner's sugar) into a bowl.
Add 3 x 5ml teaspoons of gum tragacanth.
Mix the dry ingredients together.
Add 6 x 5ml teaspoons of cold water.
Stir by hand until it becomes crumbly but damp enough to bind together. Add a little more water if it is too dry, or icing sugar if it is too wet. Turn out on to a worktop and knead until pliable.
Place into a plastic bag and leave at room temperature for 12 hours until firm.
Break off a small piece and knead between your palms. Continue kneading between your fingers. Repeat until all the paste is softened. It can be used straight away.

If you have left-over Mexican paste, wrap each piece in plastic food wrap, place all the pieces in a plastic bag and put it in the freezer. Defrost only the quantity required for each project. Smaller pieces will defrost more quickly. Store paste in an airtight container at room temperature, never in the fridge.

Flower paste

A simple flower paste can be made by mixing equal amounts of Mexican paste to sugarpaste. Ready-made and ready-coloured flower paste is available commercially.

Sugarpaste

Commercially available sugarpaste is known as fondant Icing or rolled fondant in some countries. I use it to model the hair. It can be blended and textured as it stays soft longer than Mexican or modelling paste. I use white or ivory/champagne sugarpaste for the hair before painting. For the Gothic Fairy (page 82) I used ready-made black sugarpaste.

Piping gel

This is available from sugarcraft shops. I used it as an edible glue for the tiny sugar pearls and the wafer paper wings on the Peacock Fairy (page 116), and for the water droplets in the Fairy's Bath Time project (page 90).

Confectioner's varnish

This was used for the water effect in the Fairy's Bath Time project.

Tools

The following tools are useful (but not all essential) when sculpting and modelling fairies with sugar.

Non-stick workboard Useful for kneading and rolling out paste.

Small non-stick rolling pin For rolling out paste.

Straight frill cutter This is used to make frilled edges for clothes.

Straight blade Used for making the striped effect on the dress of the Steampunk Fairy (page 102).

Ruler For measuring and cutting straight lines.

Brushpen Filled with water, this is very useful for dampening the surface of the sugar for sticking pieces together.

Angled tweezers These are used to hold elements for dipping in confectioner's varnish.

Palette knife For helping to lift paste from the workboard, mixing sticking paste, flattening paste in moulds, indenting fingers, creating texture, cutting paste, dipping less stiff elements in confectioner's varnish and spreading gelatine in moulds.

Fine pointed scissors For trimming paste and cutting details such as fingers, and for cutting edible wafer paper.

Heavy-duty scissors For cutting support sticks and wires.

Round-ended pliers Useful for shaping wires, as for the Snow Fairy's wings (page 38).

Size 0000 paintbrush For painting the finest details.

Fine paintbrush For painting the fairies.

Petal veining tool For frilling edges and adding texture.

Ball tool For marking rounded indentations.

Dresden tool Very useful for sculpting, smoothing, shaping and making lines.

Cutting wheel Cuts rolled-out paste easily without dragging. Also for marking lines on the surface of the paste.

Cutters, moulds and sticks

Commercially available moulds and cutters have been used to create some parts of the fairies and their clothes, and sticks and wires were used for strength and support. From top left:

Shaped plaque cutter Used for the Snow Fairy's bodice (page 38).

Lace wing mould These are optional but can be used for the Fairy's Bath Time project (page 90).

Multi-mould This features various tiny items including wings for the Flower Fairy's Baby (page 28).

Various **head moulds** These are used for all the fairies.

Daisy/chrysanthemum leaf cutter This is used for the My Friend the Bird project (page 50).

Blossom and heart plunger cutters These are used to make tiny details.

Piping nozzle This can be used for piping but also for indenting tiny circles, as for the bird's eyes in the My Friend the Bird project (page 50).

Snowflake cutters These are used to make decorations for the Snow Fairy (page 38).

Straight silicone petal veiner This is used to add texture to wings.

Oak leaf cutter This is used to make decorations for the My Friend the Bird project (page 50).

Plain leaf/petal cutters These are used to make decorations for many of the projects.

Tiny shoe cutters These are used for the Fairy Dressing Up project (page 72).

Star plunger cutters Used for the Snow Fairy (page 38).

Butterfly cutter This is used to make wings for the Buxom Fairy (page 16) and Dressing Up Fairy (page 72).

Silicone leaf veiner Used to add texture to leaves.

Tiny holly cutter Used for the Snow Fairy (page 38).

2.5cm (1in) carnation cutter This is used for the Buxom Fairy (page 16) and the Gothic Fairy (page 82).

Medium Christmas tree cutter This is used to make the wings of the Snow Fairy (page 38).

Garrett frill cutter Used for the Buxom Fairy (page 16).

Music stave cutter Useful for cutting thin strips of paste.

Cake pop/lolly sticks or thin bamboo kebab sticks These are used to add strength and support to fairies and to hold heads while they are being made.

18g and 33g wire Used for making the wings, and to support some of the limbs.

Colouring equipment

Edible powder food colours Plain and pearl versions are used. They can be brushed on as a dry powder or painted on mixed with pure food-grade alcohol.

Edible pen (fine and medium) These are used to draw fine details.

Pure food-grade alcohol (isopropyl alcohol) I prefer using this for painting on to sugar as there is no water which could make the sugar sticky. If it is difficult to obtain, you could use alcohol-based lemon essence, gin or vodka, but be careful as these contain water.

Gold edible paint This can be painted on straight from the bottle.

Confectioner's dusting brush A straight-sided brush holds powder colour well for dusting on edible powder food colours.

Blusher brush This can be used for dusting larger areas of paste.

Small palette box For applying small amounts of powder colour.

Other materials

Leaf gelatine For making the wings for Fairy's Bath Time (page 90) using two different methods.

Tracing paper For making templates from the patterns shown in the book.

Kitchen paper/paper tissues For mixing small amounts of powder colours and working the colour into the dusting brush. Also useful for making dress patterns for models.

Vegetable oil Use sparingly on the workboard, tools and hands to prevent paste from sticking.

Greaseproof/parchment paper For making piping bags for the piping gel if it is not already in a tube.

White florist tape For wrapping the sticks supporting some models.

Tiny edible gold and silver pearls For decoration.

Techniques

Making heads

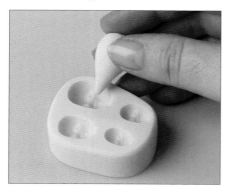

1 Roll a small piece of chestnut coloured Mexican paste into a cone and push the point into the nose part of a fairy head mould.

2 Push the paste into the mould with the end of a rolling pin.

3 Take a food-safe stick such as a kebab or cake pop stick and press it into the paste as shown.

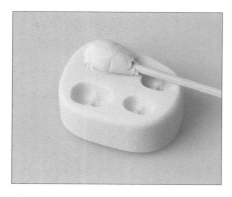

4 Bring the excess Mexican paste on to the stick to form the back of the head. Add more paste if necessary.

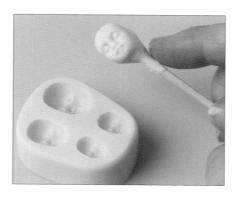

5 Take the head out of the mould, smooth down the neck and cut off any excess using scissors.

6 Leave the head to dry overnight. After this, you can add extra paste and smooth it if the head has come out of the mould lumpy.

Adding ears

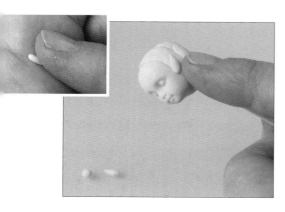

7 Roll tiny cones for ears in the same Mexican paste. Brush the sides of the head with water and press them in place.

8 Press each ear with the Dresden tool to indent it and smooth it into the side of the head.

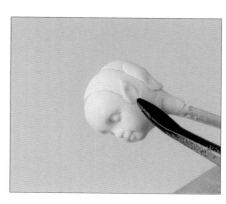

Leg without wire

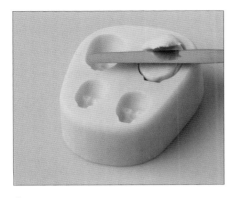

1 To measure how much Mexican paste to use for a leg, make a head in the head mould and flatten it with a small palette knife. Two flat heads make one leg.

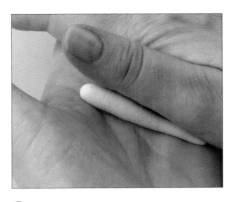

2 Roll the Mexican paste into a tapered sausage shape 6cm (2³/₈in) long.

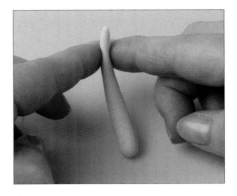

3 Roll the shape between your fingers at the pointed end to create the ankle.

Tip

All the fairy body proportions in the book are measured in this way.

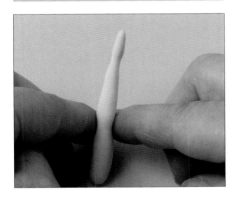

4 Halfway down the leg, roll in the same way to create the knee.

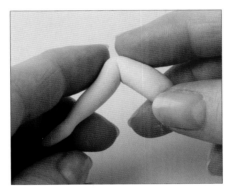

5 Bend the leg at the knee and pinch the kneecap forwards between your fingers.

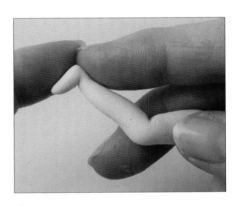

6 Pinch again to flatten the foot and create the heel.

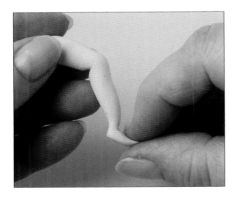

7 Stroke the toes between your finger and thumb to curve them up a little.

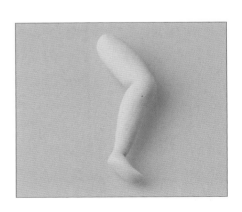

The finished fairy leg.

Wired leg

Many of the figures can be made without wires in the limbs, but when a little extra support is needed (if the arm or leg is lifted away from the body or something is held in the hand), a wire will help prevent breakage.

1 Place the ball of Mexican paste on a 33 gauge wire.

2 Roll to make a tapered sausage shape. Complete the steps as for the non-wired leg.

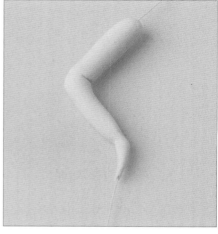

The finished fairy leg.

Arm without wire

1 Half a flat head is enough Mexican paste for one arm. Roll it to a 3cm (1¼in) tapered sausage.

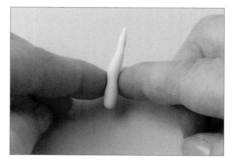

2 Roll it between your fingers to create a wrist, and then halfway down again to create an elbow.

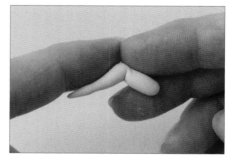

3 Bend the arm in the middle and pinch it between your fingers at the elbow.

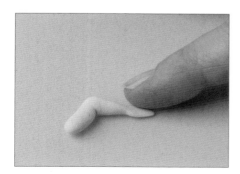

4 Flatten the hand down on to the work surface with your finger.

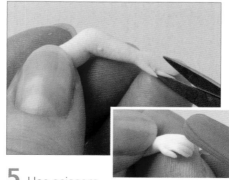

5 Use scissors to cut out a tiny 'v' shape to make the thumb, then take a palette knife to make indents, one in the middle, then one either side, to create the fingers. Push the ends to round off the fingers.

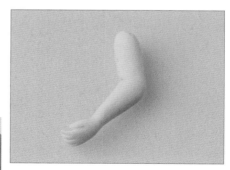

The finished fairy arm.

Wired arm

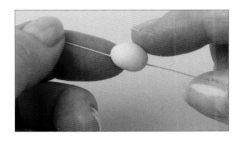

1 Place the ball of Mexican paste on a 33 gauge wire. Roll to a 3cm (1¼in) sausage shape and continue steps as for the non-wired arm opposite.

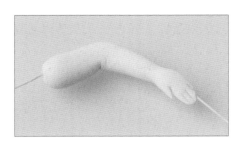

The finished fairy arm.

Wired wing

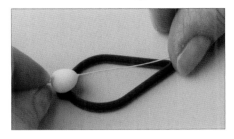

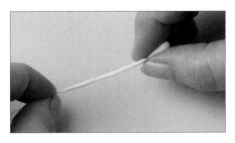

1 Put a small ball of Mexican paste on a 33 gauge wire. Measure the length of the leaf/petal cutter you are using for the wing.

2 Pinch the paste and twiddle it up the wire with your fingers to coat the length required.

3 When the wire is evenly coated, pull the excess off the end.

4 Roll out Mexican paste thinly and cut out the wing with the leaf/petal cutter. Stick the coated wire in the centre.

5 Press the wing in a petal veiner. This conceals the wire and creates texture.

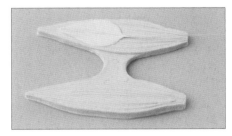

Hair

Use sugarpaste for hair as it stays soft for longer than many other modelling pastes.

1 Roll tiny balls of white sugarpaste to 2.5cm (1in) tapered sausages. Flatten them and use a palette knife to mark texture along the length.

2 Shape each piece into a lock of hair.

3 Dampen the head and press each lock in place to create the fairy's hairstyle. Use the Dresden tool to blend them in and to reinstate the texture.

Buxom Fairy

I love this cuddly fairy. She was inspired by the curvy 'bathing belles' from old English seaside postcards. She has a weakness for eating cakes and chocolates. Full of character and proud of her curves, she only has small wings, as she can't really be bothered to fly anywhere. I have added cakes and chocolates to the cake shown in the photograph, but you can design your own based on your favourites, or those of the person receiving the cake.

You will need

White Mexican paste
Baby face mould
Rolling pin
Two kebab or cake pop sticks
Edible powder food colours: autumn leaf, paprika, peach pearl, light blue, pearly pink, black, pearl white, pearl vanilla mist, pearl crushed pine, pearl Pacific blue
Water brushpen
Size 0000 paintbrush
Edible pen: coffee and black
Pure food-grade alcohol
White sugarpaste
Dresden tool
Gold edible paint
Ball tool
Polystyrene block
Heavy-duty scissors
Flat paintbrush
Confectioner's varnish
White non-toxic, non-edible hologram glitter
Confectioner's dusting brush
Paper tissue
Cocktail stick
1.25cm (½in) blossom plunger cutter
Petal veining tool
White flower paste
Garrett frill cutter
2.5cm (1in) circle cutter
3cm (1¼in) leaf/petal cutter
Silicone petal veiner
Butterfly cutter
Tweezers
Hand mould
2.5cm (1in) carnation cutter
Music stave cutter

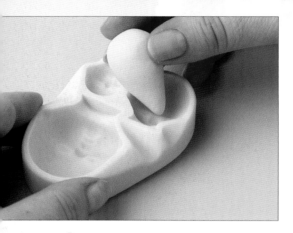

1 Use white Mexican paste kneaded together with paprika and autumn leaf edible powder food colours. Roll a cone and push the point into the nose of the baby face mould.

2 Push the paste into the mould with the end of a rolling pin.

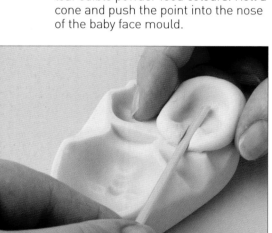

3 Press in a kebab or cake pop stick. Remove the head from the mould.

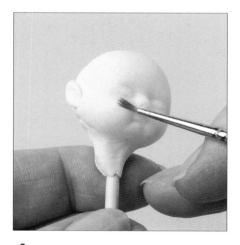

4 Shape the back of the head and leave it to dry overnight. Attach ears (see page 12). Dust the cheeks with a little peach-coloured pearl edible powder food colour on a dry brush.

The chocolates and cakes were made with Mexican paste. Plates were first cut out with a small circle cutter. The Battenberg cake was shaped by hand to an oblong; the squares painted on using food colours. Doughnuts were cut using two different sized tiny circles, painted with autumn leaf food colour, and sprinkled with icing sugar. The box of chocolates was made by cutting two small squares of paste; one of them cut into four even strips stuck on upright to the other square to form the sides of the box and painted with edible gold paint. A strip of paste painted with edible metallic food paint forms the ribbon. Chocolates were formed by using tiny shaped cutters or shaping by hand, painted with chocolate brown food colour and glazed with confectioner's varnish or piping gel. The square chocolate cake was simply rolled-out chocolate-coloured paste, cut to a small square shape and glazed as for the chocolates. For the sponge, four circles of paste were cut: one white, one red and two cream. The layers were stuck together and topped with tiny handmade swirls and berries.

5 Use a coffee-coloured fine edible pen to draw the top eyelash lines and the eyebrows.

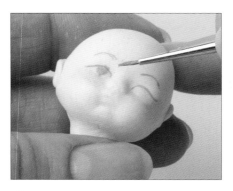

6 Paint the irises with the paintbrush and light blue edible powder food colour mixed with pure food-grade alcohol.

7 Use the coffee edible pen to paint the lower eyelash line.

8 Paint a little heart for the lips with pearly pink edible powder food colour mixed with pure food-grade alcohol.

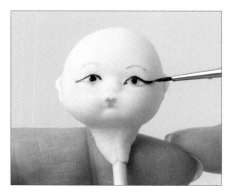

9 Paint the pupils and top eyelash lines with black edible powder food colour mixed with pure food-grade alcohol.

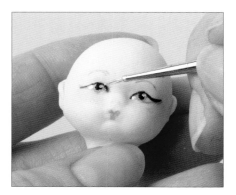

10 Use pearl white edible powder food colour mixed with pure food-grade alcohol to paint the whites of the eyes and the highlights.

11 Make locks of hair from white sugarpaste as shown on page 15 and gradually build up a Marilyn Monroe hairstyle.

12 Refine the texture of the hair with the Dresden tool.

13 Paint the hair with pearl vanilla mist edible powder food colour mixed with alcohol.

14 Add highlights with gold edible paint.

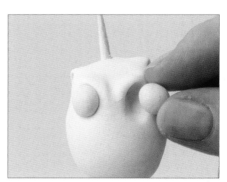

15 Make the body from four flat heads (see page 13) of the coloured Mexican paste. Form into an oval 4cm (1⁵⁄₈in) long and 3cm (1¼in) wide and push on a stick, leaving space for the head. Push in the ball tool to create arm sockets.

16 To create the bust, make two holes with the ball tool and push them upwards. Push down with your thumb and then the tool to make the cleavage.

17 Next, fill the two holes with balls of Mexican paste.

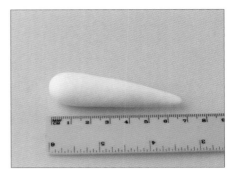

18 Trim off the bottom of the stick as shown with heavy-duty scissors.

19 Push the body into a block of polystyrene, leaning back a little, ready to assemble the fairy.

20 Make each leg from two flat heads of white Mexican paste formed into a tapered sausage 7cm (2¾in) long.

21 Shape the legs as shown on page 13. Dust pearl crushed pine edible powder food colour, on to a paper tissue, then on to the legs while the paste is still fairly soft. Use a flat, dry paintbrush.

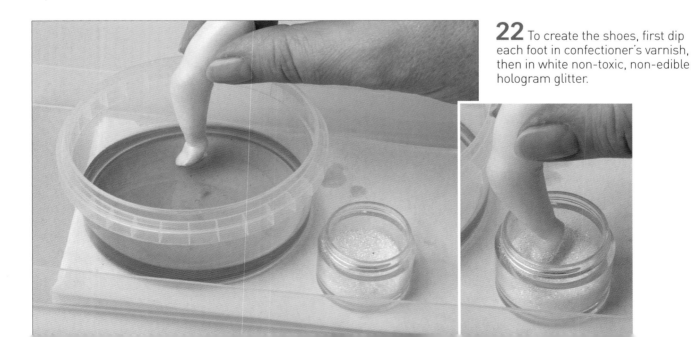

22 To create the shoes, first dip each foot in confectioner's varnish, then in white non-toxic, non-edible hologram glitter.

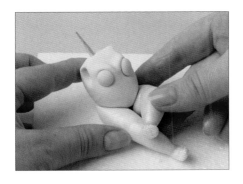

23 Brush water on the leg sockets and push on the legs, crossing one over the other as shown. Prop up the lifted leg with a cocktail stick while it dries.

24 To make the flowers for the shoes, roll out white Mexican paste and cut out six flowers with a 1.25cm (½in) blossom plunger cutter. Dust them with pearl Pacific blue edible powder food colour. Frill the edges with a petal veining tool. Layer them one right side up, one upside down and one right side up on top. Use the petal veining tool to push down the middle of each flower to attach the layers.

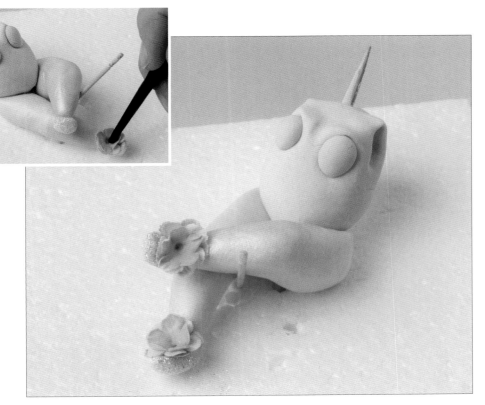

25 Brush a little water on the shoes and push a flower on to each.

26 Use a garrett frill cutter to cut out three shapes in white flower paste for the fairy's skirt, and cut out the centre of each with a 2.5cm (1in) circle cutter. Dust the fluted edges of the shapes with pearl Pacific blue edible powder food colour.

27 Frill the edges of each layer with a petal veining tool.

28 Make a cut from the centre to the outside, and gather the piece as shown.

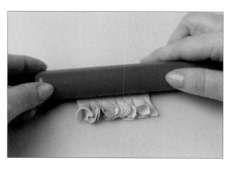

29 Flatten the circle into a line of gathers as shown and roll the unfrilled edge flat with a rolling pin. Do this for all three skirt layers.

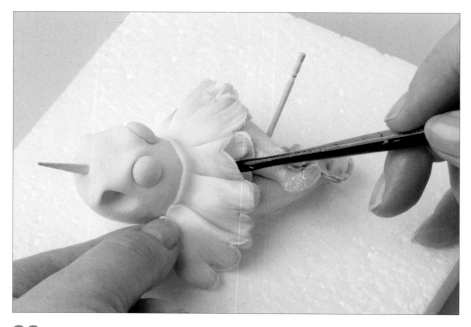

30 Trim the skirt layers along the flattened part so that they are around 2.5cm (1in) deep. Brush water around the fairy's waist and on the backs of the flattened parts of the skirt layers, and attach them using the Dresden tool to push them into place.

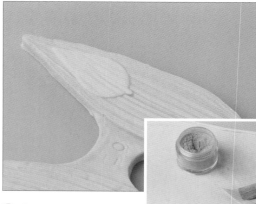

31 For the bodice, roll out white flower paste and use a 3cm (1¼in) leaf/petal cutter to cut out twelve shapes. Use the silicone petal veiner to texture them all. Dust the shapes with pearl crushed pine edible powder food colour.

32 Dampen the backs of the shapes and stick them to the fairy to hide the top of the skirt, with the leaf points facing downwards.

34 To make the wings, roll out white flower paste and leave it to dry for a while, then cut out the wings with a butterfly cutter. Dust the wings with the pearl crushed pine and Pacific blue edible powder food colours from a paper tissue as before.

33 Continue attaching the bodice shapes round to the back of the fairy.

35 Use tweezers to dip the butterfly in confectioner's varnish. Pat dry with a paper tissue and then sprinkle with the same hologram white glitter used on the shoes. Use the petal veining tool to pick up the glitter.

36 To make an arm, use half a flat head in the flesh-coloured Mexican paste as before. Roll it to a 5cm (2in) tapered sausage and press the narrow end into a hand mould. Push it down slightly with the Dresden tool. Roll and pinch as shown on page 14. Make a pair, one left and one right.

37 Roll out white flower paste and cut three flowers for each sleeve with a 2.5cm (1in) carnation cutter. Dust the edges with pearl Pacific blue edible powder food colour.

38 Frill with the petal veining tool on the fringed edges.

39 Layer the carnations as for the flowers on the shoes, with the middle one upside down. Brush the arm sockets with water and push the flowers in with the ball tool. Repeat the other side and fluff up the sleeve decorations. Push the right arm in place with the hand on the base.

40 By this time, the confectioner's varnish coating on the wings should be tacky. Dampen the fairy's back in the centre and stick the wings on, pressing with the Dresden tool.

41 Remove the head from the stick. Before pushing the head on to the body, you might need to trim the end of the stick emerging from the body, and even the neck itself. Keep trying it and trimming until it is right.

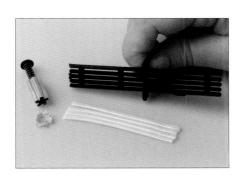

42 To make the choker, roll out flower paste and dust it with pearl white edible powder food colour, then cut it with the music stave cutter. Make a flower decoration as shown on page 21 for the shoes.

43 Brush the neck with water and attach one strip, then the flower.

44 Brush the left arm socket with water and push on the arm. Dampen the hand and push it into the hair to finish.

This page and opposite
Details of the Buxom Fairy.

Flower Fairy's Baby

This sweet little baby fairy looks so sleepy and comfortable in his nest. It would have been lovingly built by birds who raised their little brood, and left it in the tree when the baby birds flew away. Fairies will often make use of things which are no longer needed – they are very good at recycling! Page 7 shows the same fairy and nest but on a cake painted with a tree design. For the cake shown opposite, I painted the sugarpaste with orange and brown edible powder food colour and added leaves to the iced cake board.

You will need

White Mexican paste

Baby head mould

Kebab or cake pop stick

Edible powder food colours in paprika, autumn leaf, pearl peach, pearl soft pink, dark brown, chocolate brown, eucalyptus, pearl lemon sorbet, purple, yellow, foliage green

Dresden tool

Water brushpen

Size 0000 paintbrush

Pure food-grade alcohol

Coffee edible pen

Ball tool

Fine pointed scissors

Palette knife

White sugarpaste

6cm (2³⁄₈in) circle cutter

Rolling pin

Paper tissues

Confectioner's dusting brush

Cutting wheel

Wing mould

Leaf/petal cutter

White flower paste

Blossom plunger cutters

1cm (³⁄₈in) leaf/petal cutter

Silicone leaf veiner

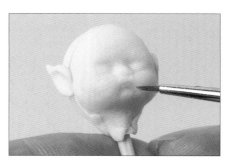

1 Use white Mexican paste kneaded together with paprika and autumn leaf edible powder food colour. Make the head as on page 12 from the 1cm (³⁄₈in) baby head mould, and add ears. Dust the cheeks with pearl peach edible powder food colour with a dry size 0000 paintbrush. Mix pearl soft pink powder with pure food-grade alcohol and paint the lips.

2 Paint the eyelash line with coffee edible pen. The baby's eyes are closed so there is just one eyelash line for each.

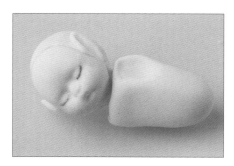

3 Make the body from two flat heads formed into a 2cm (³⁄₄in) oval and push in arm sockets with the small end of the ball tool. Remove the stick, dampen the base of the neck and push the head on to the body.

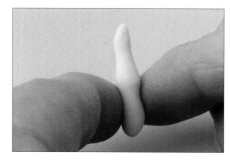

4 Make arms from half a flat head each, rolled to 2cm (³⁄₄in) long and shaped as on page 14.

5 Cut the thumbs and indent the fingers as on page 14 and curl over the fingers. Dampen the arm sockets and push on the arms as shown.

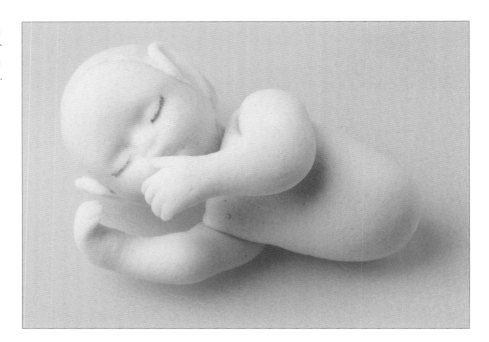

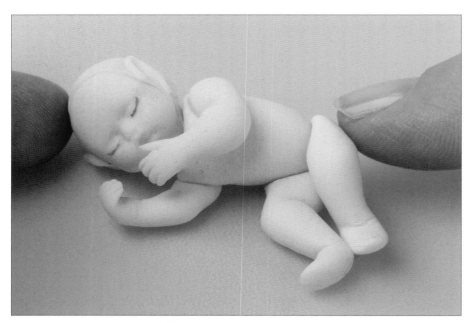

6 Make the legs from one flat head each and roll them to 3cm (1¼in) long. Shape them as on page 13. Dampen the base of the body and push on the legs as shown.

7 Make hair from white sugarpaste as shown on page 15 and texture it using a palette knife. Brush the baby's head with water and position the locks of hair. Texture and curl them.

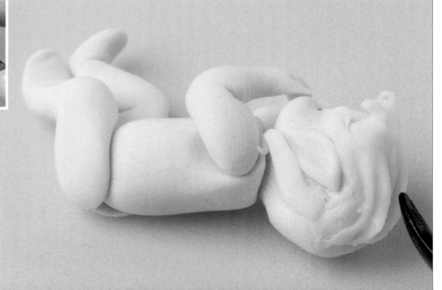

30

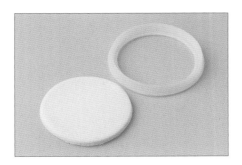

8 Make a base for the nest with 5mm (¼in) thick Mexican paste cut into a 6cm (2³⁄₈in) circle.

9 Colour Mexican paste with autumn leaf edible powder food colour and roll it out thinly. Brush it with dark brown, chocolate brown and eucalyptus powders and brush both sides of the Mexican paste with streaks as shown.

10 Use a cutting wheel to cut wiggly strips to create the twigs of the nest.

11 Take a few of the strips and twist them together.

12 Brush the edges of the circle with water and begin to place the twisted twigs to build up the nest.

13 Continue building up the nest, covering the whole base, and push down the middle with a ball tool.

14 Knead some autumn leaf edible powder food colour into white Mexican paste and push it into a wing mould. Make two of the same wing. Dust both wings with dark brown powder colour.

16 Dust the feathers with dark brown edible powder food colour. Make three feathers.

15 Roll out the same coloured Mexican paste thinly, and allow it to dry a little on both sides. Cut out feathers using the leaf/petal cutter. Mark the central rib with a Dresden tool and indent the side markings.

17 Brush on water and feather your nest!

18 Mix pearl lemon sorbet edible powder food colour with pure food-grade alcohol and paint on to the hair with the size 0000 brush.

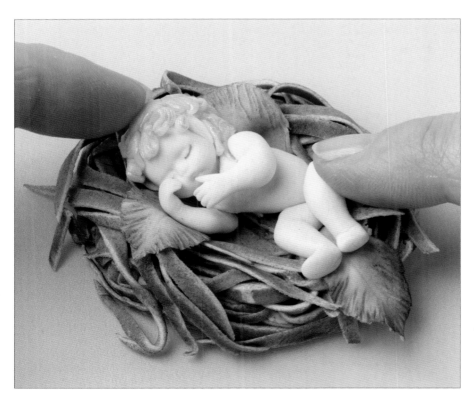

19 While the nest is still slightly soft, put the baby in it. At this stage it should nestle down as the nest settles a little.

20 To stick on the wings, use a palette knife to mix the same colour Mexican paste with a little water to make a sticking paste.

21 Apply a little sticking paste to the backs of the wings.

22 Push the wings on to the baby, with both the feathered sides upwards.

23 Roll white flower paste thinly and dust it with patches of purple and yellow edible powder food colours.

24 Use blossom plunger cutters in various sizes to cut out flowers.

25 Roll autumn leaf coloured Mexican paste thinly and use a 1cm (³/₈in) leaf/petal cutter to cut out leaves. Place them along the central vein of a silicone petal veiner and use it to impress texture.

26 Brush the leaves with foliage green powder colour. Dampen the backs of the leaves and flowers and stick them on to the nest. You can save some for the surface of the cake itself.

This page and opposite
Details of the Flower Fairy's Baby.

Snow Fairy

This tall, elegant fairy reminds me of a long shard of ice, or a tall, snow-covered fir tree in a wintry landscape. She has an air of importance and authority as she oversees her frozen, sugary dominions. Her gown shimmers with pearly holly leaves, tiny stars and snowflakes.

You will need

Cake pop or lolly stick

Mexican paste: white and chestnut

Palette knife

Edible powder food colours: pearl crushed pine, pearl white, pearl soft pink, black, iridescent green fusion, iridescent lilac fusion

Water brushpen

Blusher brush

Paper tissue

Clear piping gel

White non-toxic, non-edible hologram glitter

Petal veining tool

Fairy head mould

Kebab stick

Ball tool

White modelling paste

Size 0000 paintbrush

Pure food-grade alcohol

Coffee edible pen

Dresden tool

Rolling pin

3cm (1¼in) holly cutter

Tiny piping bag

Tiny silver edible stars

Piping gel

Plaque cutter

Tiny star plunger cutter

White sugarpaste

Fine pointed scissors

1.25cm (½in) and 2cm (¾in) snowflake cutters

24 gauge turquoise wire

Cocktail stick

Round-ended pliers

Christmas tree cutter

Cutting wheel

Heavy-duty scissors

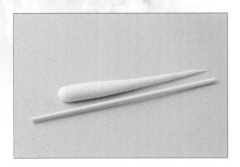

1 To make the Christmas trees, take a cake pop or lolly stick. Make a ball of Mexican paste and roll it to a long cone just shorter than the stick.

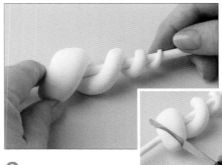

2 Hold the stick and twirl the long cone round it. Cut off the bottom of the Christmas tree with a palette knife. Dry the Christmas tree overnight and take out the stick.

3 Dust the tree with pearl crushed pine edible powder food colour using a blusher brush.

4 Pipe the edges of the twisting tree with clear piping gel. Hold it on the stick. Pick up white non-toxic, non-edible hologram glitter in a petal veining tool and sprinkle it on for highlights. Use paper tissue to catch excess glitter.

5 Make a head using chestnut-coloured Mexican paste and the largest of four fairy head moulds. Make the body from four flat heads, roll into a ball, then roll across the middle with your little finger to make a peanut shape.

6 Flatten the shape slightly between your hands.

7 Push in arm sockets with the large end of the ball tool, then push them upwards to create the shoulder. Allow to dry.

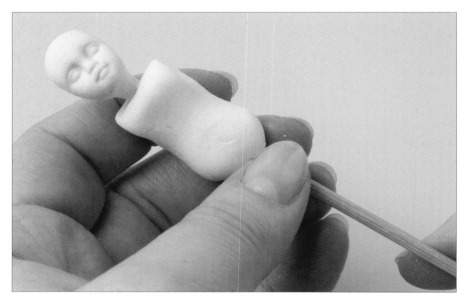

8 Push the body up a kebab stick with the head.

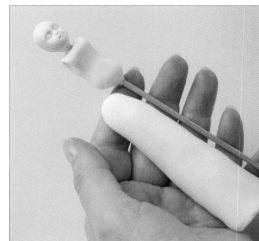

9 Use modelling paste for the skirt of the dress. Work out the size by rolling a shape as shown and measuring it against the fairy body. It should be about 10cm (4in) high.

10 Dampen the stick with water and wrap the skirt round it.

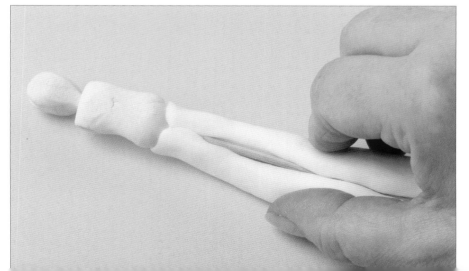

11 Stand the fairy up in a polystyrene block. Use a blusher brush to dust her with pearl white edible powder food colour.

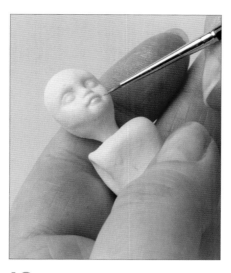

12 Mix pearl soft pink edible powder food colour with pure food-grade alcohol and use a size 0000 paintbrush to paint the fairy's lips.

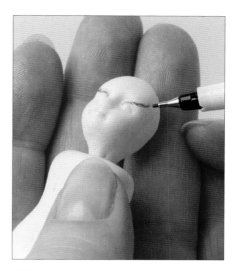

13 Draw the top eyelash lines with coffee edible pen.

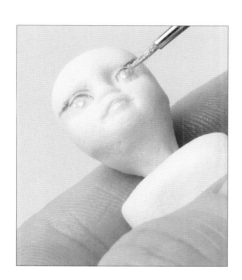

14 Paint the whites of the eyes with pearl white edible powder food colour mixed with pure food-grade alcohol. Mix pearl crushed pine edible powder food colour with food-grade alcohol in the same way and paint this on to create the fairy's irises.

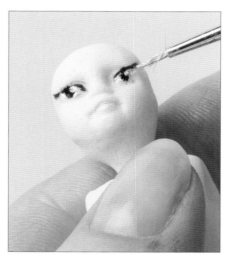

15 Mix black edible powder food colour in the same way and paint on the pupils and top eyelashes. Then paint the whites of the eyes and highlights with pearl white powder mixed with pure food-grade alcohol.

16 Make ears with the chestnut coloured Mexican paste and press them on with the Dresden tool as shown on page 12.

17 Roll out Mexican paste thinly and dust it with pearl white edible powder food colour. Cut out holly leaves with a 3cm (1¼in) holly cutter, indent a line down the centre of each with a Dresden tool and fold over.

18 Brush water on the base of the skirt and push on the holly leaves at an angle using the Dresden tool.

19 Stick on a second row of holly leaves and continue up the skirt.

20 Continue to the top of the skirt, changing the angle as you go.

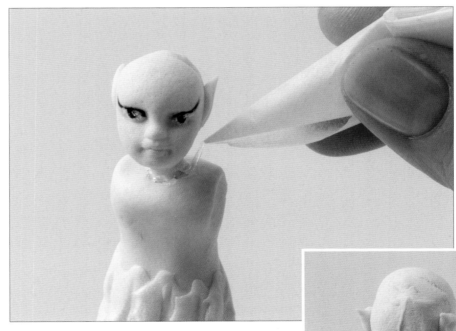

21 Decorate the neck of the fairy with tiny silver edible stars. First put piping gel in a tiny piping bag and pipe a line of gel around the neck. Dip a cocktail stick in piping gel and use it to pick up the tiny edible stars. Place them around the neck.

22 Roll out Mexican paste and dust it with iridescent green fusion edible powder good colour. Cut out a bodice shape with a plaque cutter and use the edge of the cutter to cut off the lower edge.

23 Dampen the middle of the figure and push on the bodice.

24 Overlap the edges at the back and push them in place.

25 Roll out Mexican paste and dust with iridescent lilac fusion edible powder food colour. Dampen the top and bottom of the bodice. Punch out stars using a plunger cutter and push on to the damp parts of the bodice.

26 Decorate the top and bottom of the bodice in this way.

27 Make hair from sugarpaste as on page 15. Dampen the head and place the locks of hair pointing upwards.

28 Paint the hair with iridescent lilac fusion edible powder food colour mixed with pure food-grade alcohol, then apply tiny edible silver stars as for the necklace.

29 Make arms from half a flat head of chestnut-coloured Mexican paste, following the instructions on page 14. Dampen the fairy's arm sockets and waist and place the arms with the hands on the waist.

30 Roll out Mexican paste, dust it with iridescent lilac fusion powder and leave it to dry for a while. Use 1.25cm (½in) snowflake cutter to cut out two snowflakes and cut them in half.

31 Dampen the shoulders and place the half snowflakes as sleeves. Layer the second halves on top and raise to fluff them up.

32 Make larger snowflakes using a 2cm (¾in) cutter.

33 Brush water on the back of the snowflakes and place three on the dress, coming down as shown.

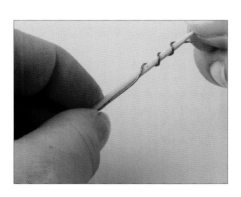

34 Take two pieces of 24 gauge turquoise wire and wind the last 2.5cm (1in) round a cocktail stick to create a spiral, or shape using round-ended pliers.

35 Roll out white Mexican paste thinly and use a cutter to cut out a Christmas tree. Cut this as shown using a cutting wheel to make two wings.

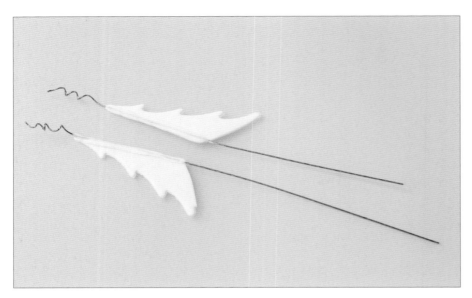

36 Twiddle Mexican paste down the wire the length of the wing, brush with water and attach the wings to make wired wings as shown on page 15.

37 Roll more Mexican paste, dust it with iridescent lilac powder and make tiny stars with a plunger cutter as for the bodice on page 43. Line the flat edges of the wings with clear piping gel, then place the stars straight from the plunger cutter.

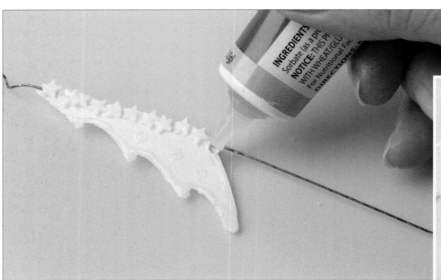

38 Squeeze piping gel along the jagged edges of the wings, and add dots. Use the petal veining tool to sprinkle on white non-toxic, non-edible hologram glitter to add sparkle to the wings.

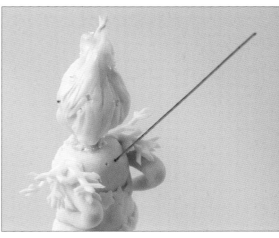

39 Bend the wire a little to curve the wings back, then make a sharp 90 degree bend at the bottom of the Christmas tree shape so that the wire can be pushed into the fairy. Trim as shown using heavy-duty scissors.

40 Use a straight wire to make two holes in the fairy's back, ready for the wings. Angle the wire as shown, pointing downwards.

41 Stick in the wings. Dot piping gel on the spiral ends of the wires and stick on little stars as in step 37. Cut out another snowflake from dusted Mexican paste as in step 30, and place this between the wings on the fairy's back to disguise the join.

This page and opposite
Details of the Snow Fairy.

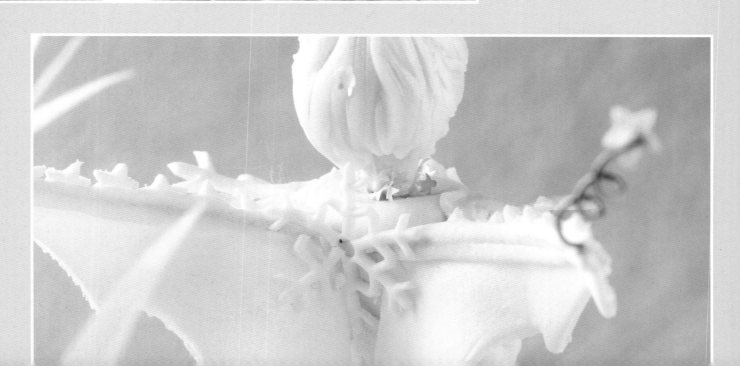

My Friend the Bird

Toddler fairies are perfectly camouflaged with leaves so that they can be safely hidden, as they are not yet skilled at flying. For this reason it is very rare to see young fairies. This little chap looks as though he is trying to whistle to the bird. When this toddler appeared, it reminded me of an ornament my mother had when I was a child.

You will need

Mexican paste in white, autumn gold, gooseberry and brown

Red sugarpaste

6cm (2³/₈in) circle cutter

Palette knife

Kebab or cake pop sticks

White sugarpaste

Water brushpen

Rolling pin

Cutting wheel

Petal veining tool

Clear piping gel

Edible powder food colours: white, soft pink, peach, pearl crushed pine, black, chocolate brown, dark brown, paprika

Size 0000 paintbrush

Cocktail stick

1cm (³/₈in) leaf/petal cutter

Size 1.5 piping nozzle

Fairy hand and foot mould

Baby head mould

Confectioner's dusting brush

Dresden tool

Pure food-grade alcohol

Coffee and black edible pens

Ball tool

Chrysanthemum leaf cutter

Silicone leaf veiner

33 gauge wire

Oak leaf cutter

Foam pad

1 Make a ball of Mexican paste and flatten it to make a dome 5cm (2in) across.

2 Cut out a circle of red sugarpaste with a 6cm (2³/₈in) cutter, lay it over the dome and stretch it down to make the cap of the toadstool.

3 Push a kebab or cake pop stick through the centre of the cap to make a hole. Texture the base of the cap with a palette knife to create radiating lines.

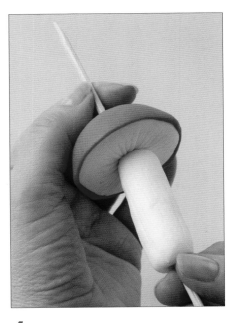

4 Make a wide sausage of Mexican paste and push this and the cap on the stick. For ease of working, push the stick into a polystyrene block.

5 Roll a long sausage of white sugarpaste, roll it flat then cut it to 1cm (³/₈in) wide with a cutting wheel. Measure round the stalk and add a bit for the overlap and cut to length. Frill one edge with the petal veining tool.

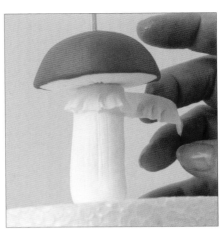

6 Dampen the frill where it is flat and stick it round the top of the toadstool stalk.

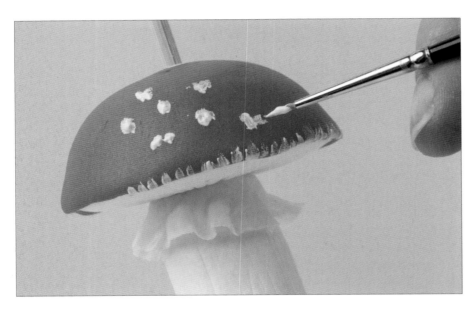

7 Mix clear piping gel with white edible powder food colour to make a paste and paint dots on the red cap of the toadstool with a size 0000 paintbrush.

8 Roll a pea-sized piece of autumn gold-coloured Mexican paste and shape it into a cone for the bird.

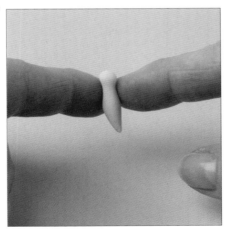

9 Roll it between your fingers just below the fat end to create the head and neck.

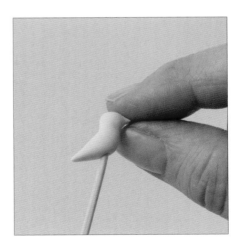

10 Pinch out the tail and beak with your finger and thumb and push the bird on a cocktail stick.

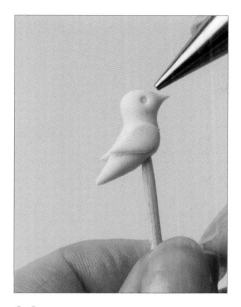

11 Roll out the same Mexican paste and cut out two 1cm (³⁄₈in) leaf/petal shapes for wings. Dampen and stick them on. Use a size 1.5 piping nozzle to make the eyes. Leave to dry.

12 Push some of the same Mexican paste into fairy hand and foot moulds. Curl the toes up a little.

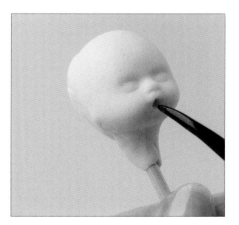

13 Push the same colour Mexican paste into the medium-sized baby head mould and make the head as on page 12. Push the pointed end of the Dresden tool in to make a hole for the mouth, and push it up a little.

14 Add ears as on page 12. Use the size 0000 brush and soft pink edible powder good colour mixed with pure food-grade alcohol to paint the lips. Dust the cheeks with peach powder and a dry confectioner's dusting brush. Use coffee edible pen to draw the eyelash lines and eyebrows, then use powder and alcohol mixes in pearl crushed pine for the eyes and black for the pupils and lashes. Draw on the hair showing beneath the hat with the coffee edible pen.

15 Make the body from four flat heads of gooseberry Mexican paste. Roll it into an oval 4cm (1½in) long. Roll between your fingers to make a bit of a waist and use a large ball tool to make the arm sockets. Thread the body on to the stick on top of the toadstool cap.

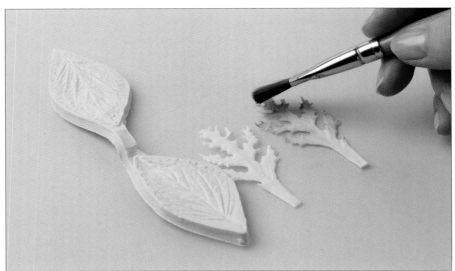

17 Roll out some gooseberry Mexican paste and cut out around twelve chrysanthemum leaves using a cutter. Press them into a silicone leaf veiner to texture them and dust them with chocolate brown edible powder food colour.

16 Remove the head from its stick, trim the body stick and push on the head, angled so that the fairy is looking up.

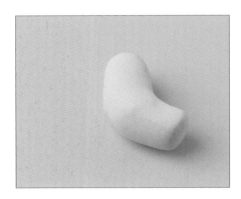

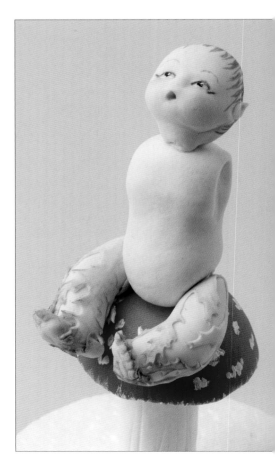

18 Using gooseberry Mexican paste, make two legs, each from one flat head.

19 Dampen the leaves and press one on either side of each leg. Dampen the base of each leg and add a foot, made in step 12.

20 Dampen and attach the legs as shown.

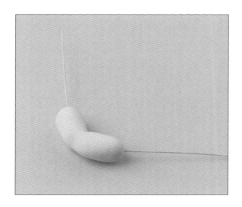

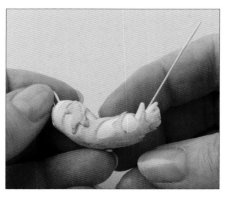

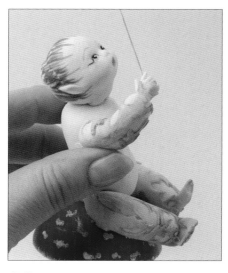

21 Make a wired arm (see page 15) from half a flat head in gooseberry Mexican paste.

22 Push a hand on so that the wire looks as though it is coming out of the finger. Dampen the back of a dusted leaf and wrap it round the arm.

23 Dampen the right-hand arm socket and stick the arm on to the body.

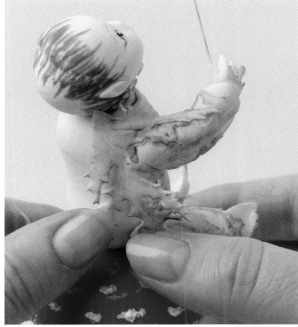

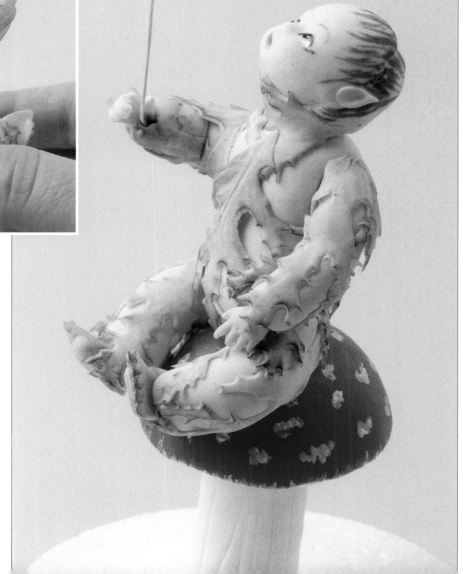

24 Make another arm in the same way but without the wire, and attach the hand. Cover the body with leaves, to decorate it and disguise the joins. Attach the second arm as shown.

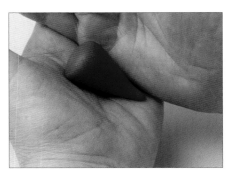

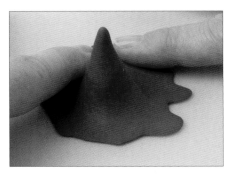

25 Make two wings with gooseberry Mexican paste rolled flat and cut with an oak leaf cutter. Add texture with a silicone leaf veiner, then frill the edges by placing the wings on a foam pad and pressing the edges with a ball tool. Dust with chocolate brown powder and leave to dry.

26 Make a cone from two flat heads of brown Mexican paste.

27 Place it on the work surface and spread it out at the base to create the hat.

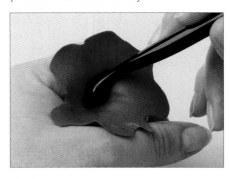

28 Hollow out the middle with a ball tool to fit the head. Try it on the head and continue until it fits.

29 Cut the edges with the chrysanthemum leaf cutter to make them ragged.

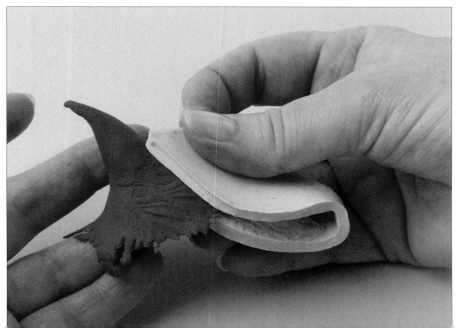

30 Press the hat with a silicone leaf veiner as shown to create texture.

31 Dust the edges of the hat with dark brown edible powder food colour to show up the texture. Dampen the inside and push it on to the head, arranging it as you prefer.

32 Dampen the wings and stick them on to the fairy's back. Curl them slightly.

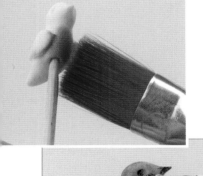

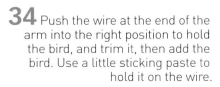

33 Dust the bird's breast with paprika edible powder food colour, and the rest of the bird with dark brown. Colour the eyes and beak with black edible pen. Remove the stick from the bird.

34 Push the wire at the end of the arm into the right position to hold the bird, and trim it, then add the bird. Use a little sticking paste to hold it on the wire.

This page and opposite
Details of My Friend the Bird.

Be My Wife

Looking deeply into each other's eyes, these fairies represent young love. Her delicately coloured lily dress and wings are beautifully complemented by his rose leaf jacket and wings – they make a perfect couple. They remind me of my very tall brother and his petite wife; she has to stand on a step to kiss him!

You will need

Mexican paste in chestnut, white, gooseberry, autumn leaf, brown

Fairy/elf mould

Kebab stick

Edible pen in coffee, blue, black and pink

Edible powder food colours in soft pink, pearl white, fuchsia pink, Cornish cream, foliage green, dark brown, rust

Pure food-grade alcohol

Paper tissue

Size 0000 paintbrush

Flat paintbrush

Confectioner's dusting brush

Water brushpen

18 gauge wire

Ball tool

Heavy-duty scissors

White 33 gauge wire

4cm (1½in), 3cm (1¼in) and 2cm (¾in) leaf/petal cutters

Silicone petal veiner

Fine pointed scissors

Dresden tool

Palette knife

White sugarpaste

Rose leaf cutters in 3 sizes, the largest 4cm (1½in)

Silcone rose leaf veiner

White 18 gauge wire

Cutting wheel

Tiny six-petal flower cutter

Petal veining/smile tool

Rolling pin

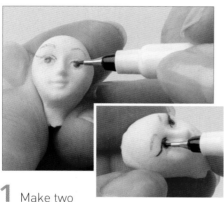
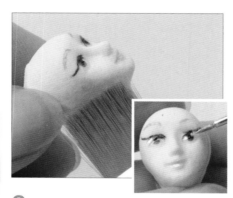

1 Make two heads from the same fairy/elf mould, from chestnut-coloured Mexican paste. Mark the girl's eyelash line and curved eyebrows with coffee edible pen, then give her irises with blue edible pen. Use a black edible pen to draw eyelashes and pupils.

2 Mix soft pink edible powder food colour with pure food-grade alcohol and use a size 0000 brush to paint the lips, then dust on the same pink for blusher with a flat, dry paintbrush. Mix pearl white edible powder food colour with alcohol as before and paint on the whites of the eyes and highlights. For painting the man's face, see step 22.

3 Make a wired leg from one flat head of white Mexican paste, using 18 gauge wire. Roll the leg to 6cm (2³/₈in) long.

4 Make the ankle and knee by rolling between your fingers. Pinch the foot forwards. Allow room on the wire for the body and head above and the mushroom below (see the finished piece opposite).

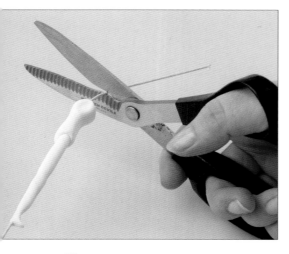

5 Make the body from two flat heads of white Mexican paste, roll it into an oval then roll between your fingers to make a peanut shape, and press to flatten it a little. Push in arm sockets with a ball tool and push it on to the wire above the straight leg. Bend the wire for the neck as the fairy is looking down, and trim the wire using heavy-duty scissors.

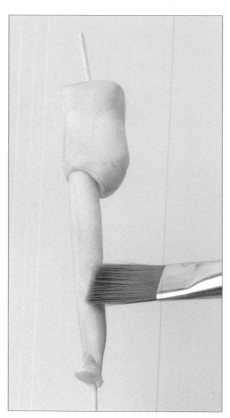

6 Dust the leg and body with fuchsia pink edible powder food colour from a paper tissue with a dry flat brush.

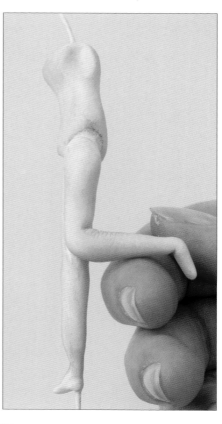

7 Make the second leg from one flat head of white Mexican paste, but without a wire as on page 13. Roll it to the same dimensions as the other leg, create the ankle and knee, dust with fuchsia pink and bend at the knee and ankle. Dampen and attach to the body. Leave the leg to dry, supporting the foot with a temporary support.

8 Make wired wings as on page 15, using white Mexican paste or flower paste and 4cm and 3cm leaf/petal cutters (two from each). Use white 33 gauge wire. Texture the wings using a silicone petal veiner.

9 Dust along the centres of the wings with fuchsia powder, and with cornish cream mixed with foliage green at the ends.

10 Roll the petal veining tool over the edges of the wings to create a frilled effect.

11 Draw on dots as for a lily petal with pink edible pen.

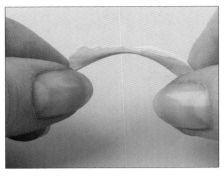

12 Use your fingers to pinch the tips of each wing and curve them. Stick them into a polystyrene block or something similar to dry.

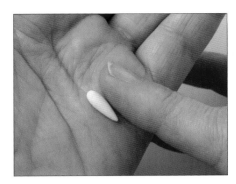

13 Roll two teardrop shapes from white Mexican paste for shoes.

14 Use the Dresden tool to shape the shoes over the fairy's feet, then clip off the ends with fine pointed scissors to trim them to size.

15 Make the mushroom cap with two flat heads of Mexican paste rolled into a ball and flattened out. Pinch into shape with a diameter of 2.5cm (1in). Use a palette knife to mark out gills on the underside. Dust the edges of the top with dark brown edible powder food colour.

16 For the stalk of the mushroom, roll one flat head of Mexican paste into a 3.5cm (1³/₈in) sausage shape. Add texture lines with the palette knife and dust with the dark brown edible powder food colour.

17 Thread the mushroom on to the wire beneath the girl and dampen the mushroom cap to help it stick. Draw on the ribbons of the girl's shoes with pink edible pen.

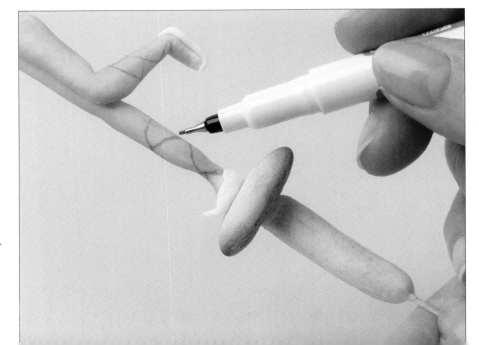

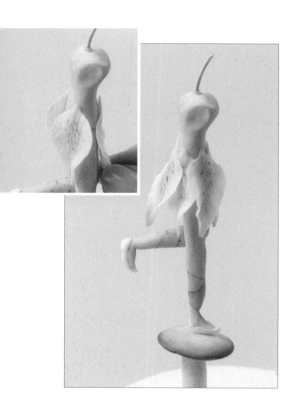

18 Prepare six lily petals for the skirt, as for the wings but without wires, using the 3cm (1¼in) leaf/petal cutter. Stand the piece in a block of polystyrene. Dampen the tops of the petals and stick them around the fairy, three first, then another layer of three.

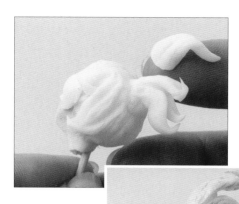

19 Add ears to the girl's head as on page 12. Make her hair from white sugarpaste, texture with the Dresden tool and push on to the dampened head going up to the pony tail tie. Then add pony tail pieces. Mix fuchsia pink and pearl white edible powder food colour with pure food-grade alcohol and paint on to the hair.

20 Trim the wire at the top of the body and position the head. This fairy should be looking down a little at her partner.

21 Attach the wings by pushing the wires into the back, with the larger ones at the top.

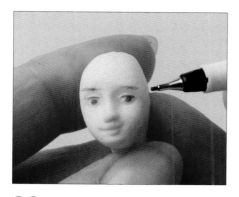

22 Paint the man's face with coffee edible pen. Make his eyebrows straight rather than curved like the girl's. Draw in the eyelash line and the irises and dust around this chin with dark brown to suggest a five o'clock shadow. Paint his lips with a very little rust edible powder food colour mixed with pure food-grade alcohol.

23 Make four wings in two different sizes using rolled out Mexican paste and two sizes of rose leaf cutter. Texture them with a rose leaf veiner. Dust them with foliage green edible powder food colour on both sides, then with dark brown powder at the edges. Pinch in the tips to make them more realistic and leave them to dry.

24 Make the body and legs of the man using a large sausage of white Mexican paste. Measure it up against the girl fairy: its top should reach her waist. It should be 1.5cm (⅝in) thick.

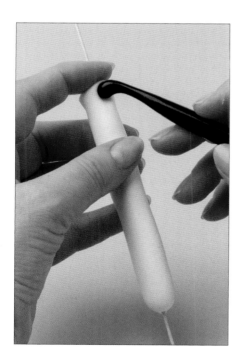

25 Push the sausage on to 18 gauge wire. Flatten it a little and make arm sockets with a ball tool.

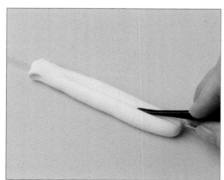

26 Mark the division for the legs on both sides with the pointed end of the Dresden tool.

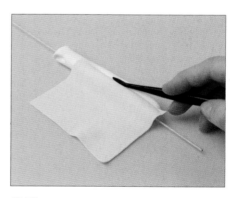

27 Roll out gooseberry Mexican paste for the trousers. Cut it to a rectangle with a cutting wheel and wrap it round the legs, starting in the gap between them. Dampen between the legs and smooth in the trousers with the Dresden tool.

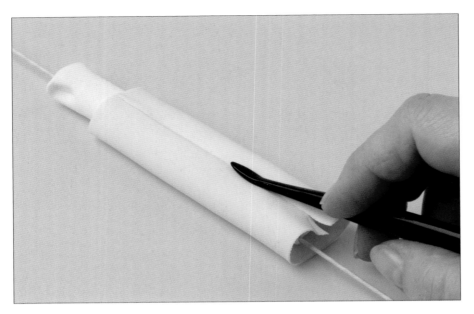

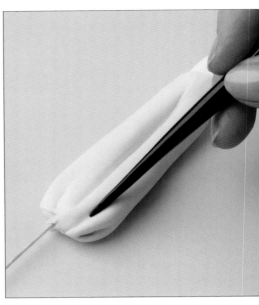

28 Trim off the excess with a cutting wheel and smooth the flap between the legs with the Dresden tool, leaving the trousers a little loose at the sides.

29 Dampen the inside of the waistband and press it in. Press in the bottoms of the trouser legs where the boots will go and add creases with the Dresden tool. Dust the trousers with foliage green edible powder food colour.

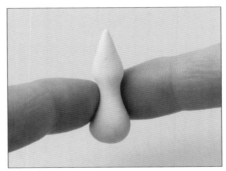

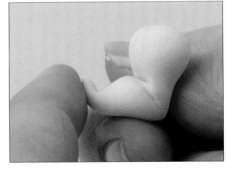

30 Make the boots from autumn leaf Mexican paste, using half a flat head for each one. Roll into a 2.5cm (1in) cone.

31 Roll between your fingers to create an ankle.

32 Bend to create the boot shape, curl up the toe and pinch out the heel.

33 Pinch out the top of each boot and use fine pointed scissors to snip out little 'v' shapes.

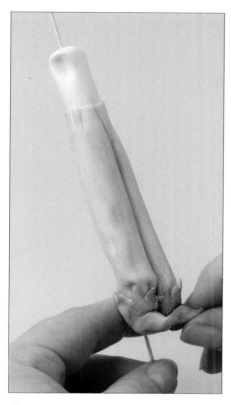

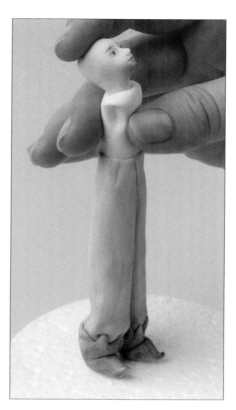

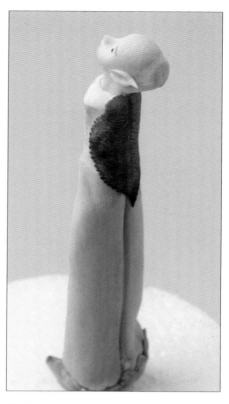

34 Dust the boots with dark brown edible powder food colour. Dampen the insides and attach them to the legs.

35 Push the man fairy into a polystyrene block. Bend back the neck wire and trim it, try the head on it and trim it again if necessary. You may need to trim the neck too. Push on the head, looking upwards at his partner.

36 Roll out Mexican paste and use a 4cm (1½in) rose leaf cutter to make three leaves for the jacket. Press them in a leaf veiner and dust them as for the wings. Dampen one and press it on to the man's back then add two at the front in the same way.

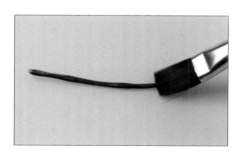

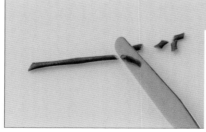

37 Make a long, very thin sausage of autumn leaf Mexican paste and dust it with dark brown edible powder food colour.

38 Cut into tiny bits of twig for buttons. Indent the front of the jacket using the Dresden tool, dampen the indentations and push in the buttons.

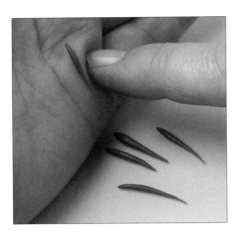

39 Make the hair from brown Mexican paste, as this is more likely to stay spiky than sugarpaste. Make tiny cones.

40 Dampen the head and press on the hair with a Dresden tool, working up a hairstyle.

41 The final stages should be done in situ. You could cover a cake blank in white sugarpaste for the final tier, and push in the figures as shown.

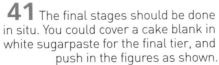

42 Make the man fairy's arms with chestnut Mexican paste, using one flat head per arm and the steps on page 14. Measure them against the two figures as they need to reach her waist. Dampen the arm sockets and the girl's waist, and push the arms in place.

43 Make two sleeves as for the smaller parts of the wings, and dampen and attach them.

44 Make sticking paste by adding water to Mexican paste and mixing with a palette knife. Stick some to the man fairy's back and stick on the wings as shown with the larger ones at the top.

45 Make arms for the girl using chestnut Mexican paste, allowing half a flat head for each. Dampen the arm sockets and the hands and place them as shown with the hands on the man's shoulders.

46 Make sleeves for her as for the wings, using a 2cm (¾in) leaf/petal cutter. Dampen them and stick them on to her shoulders. Use a tiny six-petal flower cutter to cut out eight flowers from Mexican paste, and dust them with fuchsia pink edible powder food colour. Dampen the shoes and the base of the pony tail and stick one flower on each shoe and the others around the pony tail. Use the smile tool to push them in place.

This page and opposite
Details of Be My Wife.

Fairy Dressing Up

Little children love dressing up in adult clothes – I know I did! What this little fairy sees in the mirror is a beautifully dressed grown-up fairy. While mummy fairy is away, she takes the opportunity to try on her shoes, poppy petal dress and floppy hat, and checks out her reflection in a flower mirror. The finished effect is so pretty.

You will need

Mexican paste in chestnut, autumn leaf, white

Fairy head mould

Edible pen in coffee, blue, black

Edible powder food colour in soft pink, purple, pearl pink sherbert, foliage green, primrose yellow

Confectioner's dusting brush

Paper tissue

Kebab or cake pop stick

Pure food-grade alcohol

Size 0000 paintbrush

Dresden tool

Ball tool

Water brushpen

Rolling pin

2cm (¾in) shoe cutters

0.5cm (⅛in) and 1cm (⅜in) circle cutters

Red flower paste

Large blossom plunger cutter

White sugarpaste

2.5cm (1in) heart cutter

2.5cm (1in) rose petal cuter

Petal veining/smile tool

Cotton bud

Black flower paste

Music stave cutter

Clear piping gel

Tiny piping bag

Cocktail stick

Tiny silver balls

Fine paintbrush

Gold liquid food paint

4.5cm (1¾in) five-petal flower cutter

Foam pad

Tiny butterfly cutter

Fine pointed scissors

Palette knife

Calyx cutter

2.5cm (1in) shisha mirror

24 gauge turquoise wire

Strong non-toxic craft glue

4cm (1½in) six-petal flower cutter

Small heart plunger cutter

1 Make a fairy head from the second size down in the mould, using chestnut-coloured Mexican paste (see page 12). Use coffee edible pen for the eyebrows and eyelash lines, blue pen for the irises and black pen for the pupils. Dust the cheeks with soft pink edible powder food colour.

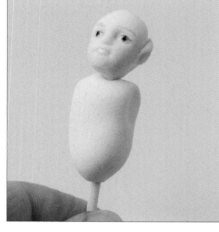

2 Paint the mouth with soft pink powder mixed with pure food-grade alcohol, using a size 0000 paintbrush. Add ears as shown on page 12. Make the body from three flat heads of the same Mexican paste rolled to a 2cm (¾in) long oval. Push in arm sockets with a ball tool and place on the stick.

3 Make two legs from the same Mexican paste, using half a flat head per leg. Shape as on page 13, to about the same length as the body. Dampen and attach them.

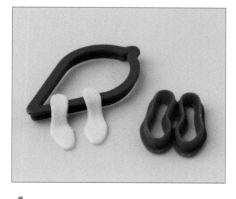

4 Roll out autumn leaf Mexican paste and use 2cm (¾in) shoe cutters to cut out two soles. Rest them over another cutter to create the high-heeled shape. Leave to dry.

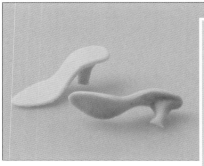

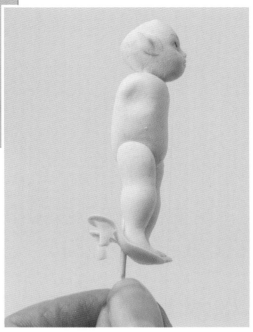

5 To make the heels, cut out 0.5cm (¹⁄₈in) circles from thickly rolled autumn leaf Mexican paste, then cut into one side with a 1cm (³⁄₈in) circle cutter. Finally, cut into the other side with the same cutter to create the heel shape.

6 Dampen the heels and stick them on to the soles, then dampen the fairy's feet and stick on the shoes.

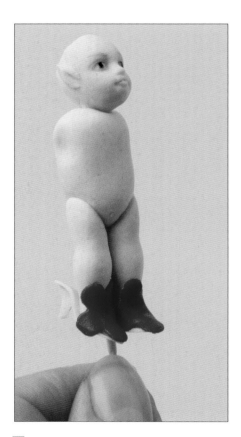

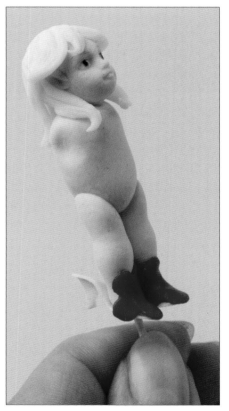

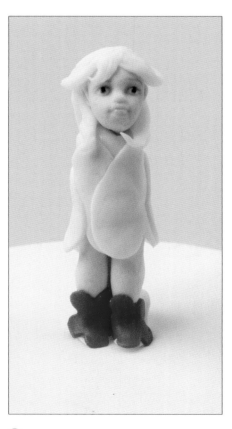

7 Roll out red flower paste thinly and allow it to dry on both sides. Use a large blossom plunger cutter to cut out the shoe tops. Dampen them and stick them to the feet.

8 Use white sugarpaste to make the hair, as shown on page 15. Make long hair, dampen the head and stick on the hair to make the little girl's hairstyle.

9 To make the petticoat, roll out white Mexican paste and use a 2.5cm (1in) heart cutter to cut four hearts. Brush them with water and stick them on to the fairy, points upwards and overlapping as shown.

10 Roll out red flower paste very thinly and allow it to dry a little on both sides. Use a 2.5cm (1in) rose petal cutter to cut out six petals and thin and frill the edges with a petal veining tool.

11 Press the petals together as shown to make the skirt.

12 Brush the fairy's waist with water and attach the skirt. She is holding up the skirt on one side so place a cutton bud or something similar to hold it up while drying.

13 Roll out black flower paste and use a music stave cutter to cut strips. Cut one strip in half and loop the ends. Press the strips together to make a bow and trim the tails at an angle.

14 Stick on the sixth petal to make the top of the dress, half covering the face (but do not stick it to the face). Stick another black strip round the waist for the belt. Trim it to fit.

15 Curl the top down and stick it to the fairy's chest. It should look too big for her as she is trying on her mother's dresses.

16 Dampen and stick on the bow at the back.

17 Put clear piping gel in a tiny piping bag and pipe the shape of the necklace on the fairy's neck and the front of her dress.

18 Dip a cocktail stick in piping gel and pick up tiny silver balls. Place these to create the necklace.

19 Use a fine paintbrush and gold liquid food paint to paint the hair.

20 Use white Mexican or flower paste for the hat. Roll it out thinly and use a 4.5cm (1¾in) five-petal flower cutter to cut out a flower. Dust the edges of both sides with purple edible powder food colour on a confectioner's dusting brush.

21 Place the flower on a foam pad and use a ball tool to frill the edges.

22 Roll out a tiny amount of white Mexican or flower paste and cut a tiny butterfly for the wings with a butterfly cutter. Dust with pearl pink sherbert edible powder food colour. Dampen and place on the back of the fairy.

23 Place the hat on the fairy and curl up the petals.

24 Make the arms from half a flat head each of chestnut Mexican paste, rolled to 2cm (¾in) long. Dampen the sockets. Dampen the hand of the first arm and place it in the socket with the arm holding the hat.

25 Dampen the hand of the second arm and place it in the socket with the hand holding up the dress.

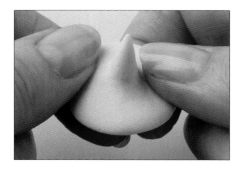

26 Make a cone from white Mexican paste for the calyx of the flower hat. Pinch out the base to flatten it.

27 Roll out the base of the calyx with the straight part of the petal veining tool or a thin rolling pin to flatten it further.

28 Cut with a calyx cutter and dust with foliage green edible powder food colour from a paper tissue.

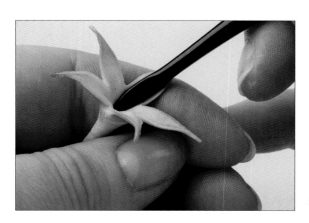

29 Hollow out the centre of the calyx with the flat end of a Dresden tool. Curl up the edges and dampen the inside.

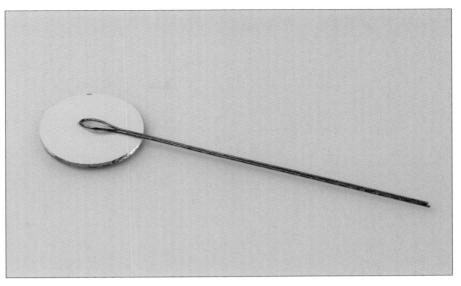

30 Stick the calyx on the flower hat.

31 To make the fairy's mirror, double a piece of 24 gauge turquoise wire and make a loop in the middle. Stick the looped end to a 2.5cm (1in) shisha mirror with strong, non-toxic craft glue. Allow to dry.

32 Roll out white Mexican paste, not too thin. Use a 4cm (1½in) six-petal flower cutter to cut out four flowers. Double up the flowers to make thicker, twelve-petal flowers. Dust each flower on both sides with primrose yellow edible powder food colour. Use a plunger cutter to cut a heart out of the middle of one of the double flowers. Attach the flowers with piping gel, the intact one on the back of the shisha mirror and the one with a heart-shaped hole on the front.

This page and opposite
Details of Fairy Dressing Up

Gothic Fairy

Bat wings and spider's webs adorn this striking fairy. The dress was inspired by a rare black iris flower. She may look stern but that's just her style; she actually has a heart of gold. Make this fairy for your favourite goth, or for a Halloween party.

You will need

Mexican paste in white
Fairy/elf mould
Kebab/cake pop stick
Black edible pen
Edible powder food colour in black
Confectioner's dusting brush
Paper tissue
Rolling pin
Cutting wheel
Black flower paste
Ball tool
Petal veining tool
33 gauge wire
White florist tape
Black sugarpaste
5cm (2in) leaf/petal cutter
2.5cm (1in) carnation cutter
Fine pointed scissors
Palette knife

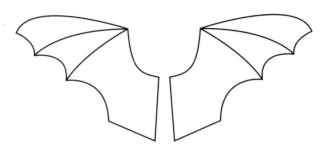

The template for the wings

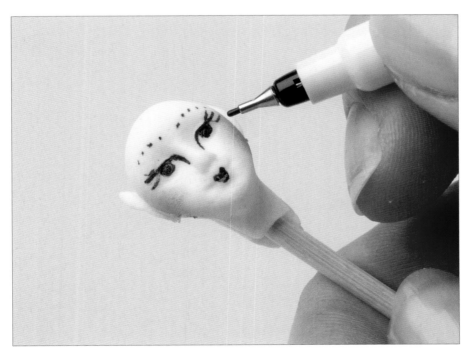

1 Make the fairy's head with white Mexican paste in the fairy/elf mould. Use black edible pen to draw the eyelash lines, eyelashes, pupils and dotted eyebrows. Add a little heart-shaped black mouth. Dust the cheeks with black edible powder food colour from a paper tissue, using a confectioner's dusting brush.

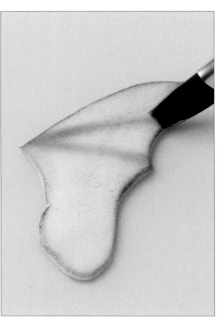

2 Roll out white Mexican paste. Use the template on page 82 to cut out a card template and cut round this to make each wing using a cutting wheel.

3 Dust around the edges of each wing with black edible powder food colour, then brush a little across the middle and create lines for the divisions as shown. Fold along the division lines and leave to dry.

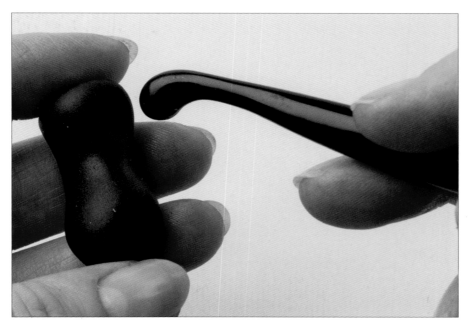

4 Make the body from four flat heads in black flower paste. Roll it between your fingers to create the waist. Pinch leg holes and push arm sockets in with a ball tool.

5 Roll out black flower paste and cut out a flower with a 2.5cm (1in) carnation cutter. Frill the edge of the carnation with the petal veining tool.

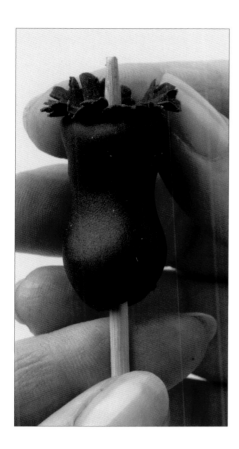

6 Push the body on a kebab or cake pop stick, and thread the black carnation on top for a collar.

7 Push the head on over the collar.

8 Make a leg on a wire as shown on page 14, using black flower paste, and attach it to the fairy as shown. Cut a thin strip of white florist tape and wrap it round the stick below the leg to hold the wire in place.

9 Stick on the second leg and dampen the insides with water to stick the legs together. You can add a little black flower paste to the feet to make it look as though the fairy is wearing shoes.

10 Make the hair from black sugarpaste as shown on page 15 and create a gothic fairy hairstyle with a widow's peak as shown.

11 Roll out black flower paste and use a 5cm (2in) leaf/petal cutter to cut out ten petals. Frill the edges with a petal veining tool.

12 Dampen the black petals and begin to place them on the figure to create her dress, beginning from the bottom near the shoes.

14 Use half a flat head of white Mexican paste to make each arm, as on page 14. Create a cobweb design for a lace sleeve and glove using black edible pen, and paint the fingernails in the same way.

13 Continue up the dress, curling and layering the petals to create the iris shape.

15 Dampen the arm sockets and press on the arms. Position them so that they are crossed, with each hand clasping the other forearm.

16 Finally, attach the wings. Make sticking paste from black flower paste mixed with water, and apply this to the wings, then position them as shown on the fairy's back.

This page and opposite

Details of Gothic Fairy.

Fairy's Bath Time

Even a fairy has to wash! Splashing about in a waterlily on a pond with droplets of water in her hair, this fairy with dragonfly wings is completely absorbed in her own thoughts. I have given you two alternative ways of making the wings.

You will need

White flower paste

Rolling pin

4cm (1½in) leaf/petal cutter

Edible powder food colours in fuchsia pink, foliage green, soft pink, iridescent gold fusion, pearl iridescent green

Confectioner's dusting brush

Paper tissue

Silicone petal veiner

Water brushpen

Tea strainer

Petal veining tool

6cm (2³⁄₈in) and 4cm (1½in) circle cutters

Cutting wheel

Black sugarpaste

20.3cm (8in) cake board

Confectioner's varnish

Cotton bud

Palette knife

Chestnut-coloured Mexican paste

Fairy head mould

Cocktail stick

Coffee edible pen

Pure food-grade alcohol

Size 0000 paintbrush

Dresden tool

White sugarpaste

Clear piping gel

Sheet of leaf gelatine

Bowls

33 gauge white wire

Bottle

Lace wing mould (optional)

Fine pointed scissors

Heavy-duty scissors

Ball tool

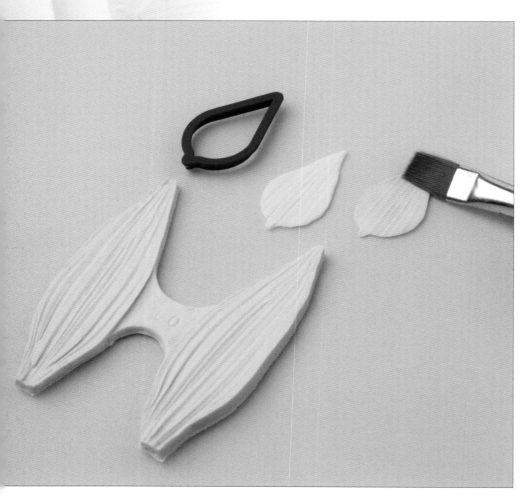

1 Roll out white flower paste to make the petals for the waterlily so that they can be drying while you continue with the project. Roll out the flower paste and use a 4cm (1½in) leaf/petal cutter to cut out the petals. Cut sixteen to twenty petals and press them in a silicone petal veiner to create texture. Dust them with fuchsia pink edible powder food colour from a paper tissue on a confectioner's dusting brush, brushing across the veins to pick up the texture.

2 Place the petals to dry over a former, in this case a tea strainer, to retain the curved shape. Dampen their ends and stick them all together to form the waterlily shape.

3 Roll out white flower paste kneaded together with foliage green edible powder food colour to create a natural look. Dry a little on both sides. Cut out some 6cm (2³⁄₈in) and some 4cm (1½in) circles using cutters and cut into them with a cutting wheel to make the lily pads. Dust from the edges with foliage green powder and then frill the edges with the petal veining tool.

4 Roll out black sugarpaste and cover a 20.3cm (8in) cake board for the lily pond. Trim the edges. Take a cotton bud and paint the lily pond with confectioner's varnish (the varnish ruins brushes).

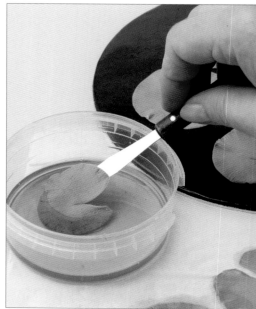

5 Dip the lily pads in the confectioner's varnish, holding them on a palette knife, and place them on the lily pond.

6 Make the girl's head from chestnut-coloured Mexican paste, using the second size down in the fairy head mould and pressing a cocktail stick into the head. Use coffee edible pen to paint her eyebrows and her eyelashes, remembering that her eyes are closed. Dust the cheeks with soft pink edible powder food colour. Mix the same powder with pure food-grade alcohol and use a size 0000 paintbrush to paint the lips.

7 Add ears as shown on page 12. Make the hair from white sugarpaste as on page 15. Twist and twirl it, because she is washing it.

8 When the glaze on the lily pond is dry, go over it with the Dresden tool to create ripples around the lily pads.

10 There are two ways of making the wings using gelatine. This first method means that you do not need to buy a lace wing mould. Soak a sheet of gelatine in a small bowl of cold water for two minutes.

9 Dampen the base of the waterlily and place it on the pond. You can prop it up with a little paper tissue if you need to retain the curved shape as it dries.

11 When the sheet has softened, place the small bowl in a bain marie as shown (in a larger bowl with boiling water in it) or in the microwave, until the gelatine is melted. Follow the directions on your gelatine packet.

12 Add a little pearl iridescent green edible powder food colour on a palette knife.

13 To wire each wing, take a 33 gauge white wire, twist it round a bottle or similar shape and twist the ends to secure it.

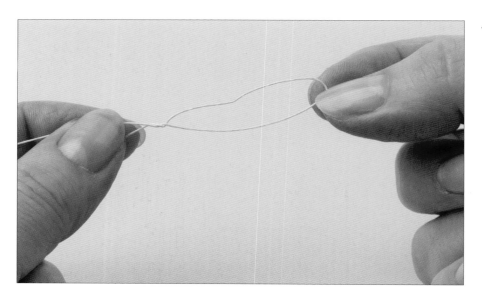

14 Pull the wire into a longer shape and make a kink in it to create a dragonfly wing.

15 Dip the wire into the gelatine mixture. It should create a film as when you dip into bubble liquid ready to blow bubbles. Allow to dry for two hours. Make two larger and two smaller wings.

16 As an alternative method for making wings, you can use a lace wing mould. Prepare the gelatine and iridescent powder in the same way and use a palette knife to spread it into the mould. Allow to dry. Make two wings in one size and two in another. Leave in a warm, dry place to dry. Once they are dry, the wings will easily peel away from the mould.

17 When the wings are dry, trim round the edges with fine pointed scissors.

18 If you have made the wired wings, trim the wires at the ends of the wings using heavy-duty scissors.

19 Make the body from four flat heads in chestnut-coloured Mexican paste. Roll between your fingers to create a peanut shape and flatten it a little. Push in arm sockets with a ball tool. Make the legs from two flat heads each and roll them to 4cm (1½in) long. Shape as on page 13 and bend them at the knee. Sit the body up and place the legs as shown.

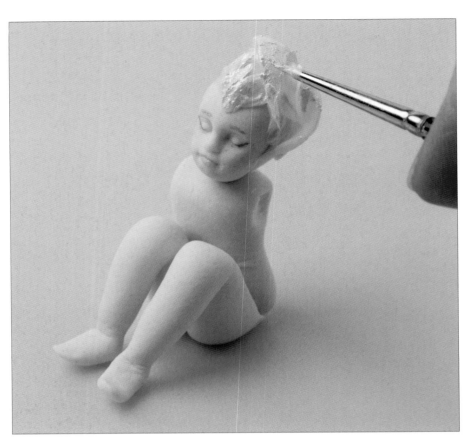

20 Attach the head to the body with a little flesh-coloured sticking paste, made as shown on page 34. Paint the hair with iridescent gold fusion powder mixed with pure food-grade alcohol, using a size 0000 paintbrush.

21 Use half a flat head for each arm, roll them to 2cm (¾in) long and shape them as on page 14. Dampen them and place them in the sockets, with the hands in the hair.

22 Put some piping gel in the middle of the waterlily to look like water, and place the fairy on top. Add more water droplets on the lily pads and on her hair in the same way.

23 Finally attach the wings, whether they are moulded or wired, with flesh-coloured sticking paste (see page 34).

This page and opposite
Details of Fairy's Bath Time.

Steampunk Fairy

Inspiration for this fairy came from some of the elements in the Steampunk fashion, which is based in the Victorian age, featuring antique clothing, imagined mechanical developments and an interest in flying. Flying goggles are an obvious help for fairies. This one is just an old-fashioned girl, but very stylish. With her striped dress, lace wings, hat and goggles, she keeps a close eye on the time on her fob-watch. She will look after your keys (but she hides them from you if you have annoyed her!)

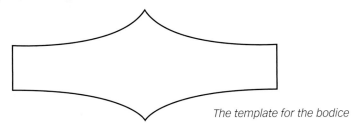

The template for the bodice

You will need

Mexican paste in chestnut, white, brown

Fairy head mould

Dresden tool

Kebab/cake pop sticks

Edible pen in coffee and black

Ball tool

Butterfly mould

Water brushpen

Edible powder food colour in pearl iridescent gold fusion

Paper tissue

Confectioner's dusting brush

Black flower paste

Rolling pin

Music stave cutter

Dresden tool

Flower paste in white, dark brown and brown

33 gauge wire

White florist tape

Frill cutter

Palette knife

Petal veining tool

Food bag

Straight blade

Cutting wheel

Tissue paper

Fine pointed scissors

2.5cm (1in) circle cutter

0.5cm (¼in) circle cutter

1cm (³/₈in) oval cutter

Gold liquid food paint

Size 0000 paintbrush

Piping gel

Tiny edible gold sugar pearls

0.5cm (¼in) square cutter

Cocktail stick

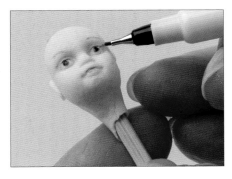

1 Make a head as shown on page 12, using chestnut coloured Mexican paste in the largest fairy head in the mould. Add ears and use coffee edible pen to draw on brows and eyelash lines. Draw irises in black edible pen.

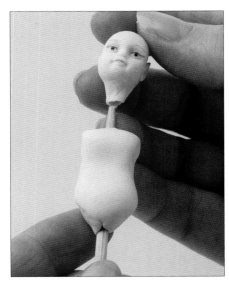

2 Make the body from four flat heads and roll it between your fingers to create a waist. Flatten a little and push in arm sockets with a ball tool. Push the body on to a kebab or cake pop stick and put the head on top.

3 Press white Mexican paste into the bottom half of a butterfly mould to create a little lace collar. Make two pieces.

4 Brush on water and press on the lace collar.

5 Push white Mexican paste into a whole butterfly mould to make the wings.

 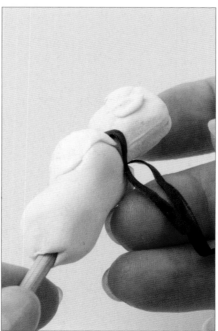 

6 Dust the wings with pearl iridescent gold fusion edible powder food colour using a confectioner's dusting brush. Place them over the corner of a box to dry.

7 Roll out black flower paste and cut using a music stave cutter. Dampen round the fairy's neck and place one of the strips round the neck as a choker. Trim to size.

8 Mix white flower paste with dark brown flower paste and use it to make hair as shown on page 15. Dampen the head and place the hair as shown.

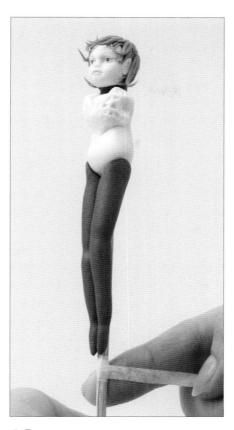

11 To make the petticoat, roll out white flower paste to a rectangle 8 x 15cm (3^1/$_8$ x 5^5/$_8$in). Lay the edge over a frill cutter and roll a rolling pin over it to make a cleaner cut.

9 Complete the fairy's hairstyle as shown.

10 Make the legs on wires, from brown Mexican paste, as shown on page 14. Make them 7cm (2¾in) long. Attach them to the dampened body on the stick. Wrap a narrow strip of white florist tape round the stick below the feet. Push the fairy into a polystyrene block or similar.

12 Frill the cut edge using a petal veining tool. Cut into two halves lengthwise. Take each half and gather it to create a concertina effect.

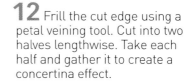

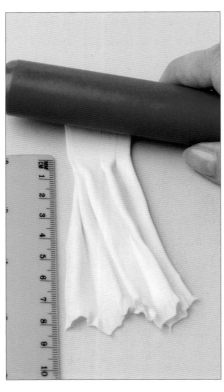

13 Measure each piece; they should be 7cm (2¾in) high. Roll the gathered tops with a rolling pin. This makes it easier to attach the petticoat pieces to the fairy. Trim them off so the total height is 8cm (3⅛in).

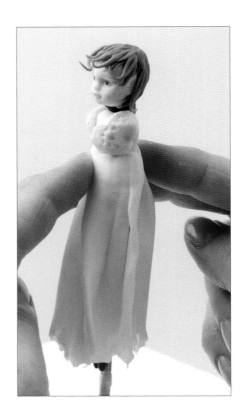

14 Dampen the insides of the flat tops and press them on to the fairy, one at the front and one at the back, lining up the sides carefully.

15 To make the stripes for the dress, first roll out brown flower paste between two sticks. This will ensure that the stripes are even. Keep it covered in a food bag so that it does not dry out.

16 Roll out black flower paste in the same way, place the black on top of the brown and trim both pieces to 6 x 10cm (2⅜ x 4in).

17 Use a straight blade to cut the rectangle in half and put one half on top of the other, then begin slicing stripes 2mm (¹/₁₆in) thick.

18 Lay the stripes side by side and push them together to meld them into a striped fabric effect.

19 Put a plastic food bag over the stripes and roll them to join them, making sure you always roll in a straight line to keep the stripes straight.

20 Lift up the piece with a palette knife. Trim it to 6.5cm (2½in) length (shorter than the petticoat) with a cutting wheel. Cut into three lengths to make it easier to work with and gather, roll and trim the tops as for the petticoat.

21 Dampen the top of each panel and place them on the fairy.

22 Continue to create the whole skirt.

23 Leave a gap at the front of the skirt to show the petticoat.

24 Make a further striped panel to decorate the front of the skirt and fold it over on the diagonal.

25 Fold it back on itself.

26 Fold the corner forwards again.

27 Fold back again as shown to complete one side.

28 Fold the other half of the panel in the same way.

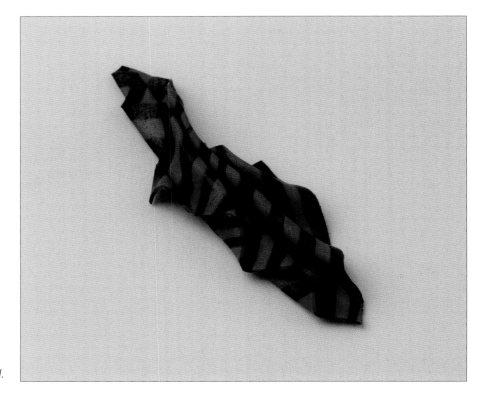

The folded panel.

29 Roll one end and trim as before. Dampen the top and attach to to the front of the fairy's skirt.

30 Roll out black flower paste for the bodice and use the template on page 102 to make a template from tissue paper. Use it to cut out the shape with a cutting wheel.

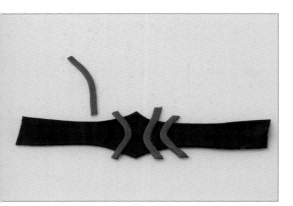

31 Roll out brown flower paste and cut using a music stave cutter. Paint water where you want stripes to go on the bodice, then place and curve brown strips and trim them to size.

32 Dampen the bodice and fit it to the figure.

33 Secure the bodice at the back and trim it to size.

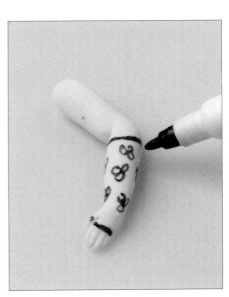

34 Make the arms from one flat head each of chestnut coloured Mexican paste. Shape them as on page 14. Paint on lace gloves with black edible pen. First paint the lines at the top and bottom, then add three-petal flowers. Add faint squiggles between the flowers to create a lace effect.

35 Dampen the arm sockets and place the arms as shown.

36 Take two more of the strips of brown flower paste that you cut in step 31 to make straps for the dress. Join each strap to a stripe at the front of the bodice and take it over the shoulder and down the back. Trim to size.

37 Roll out black flower paste, not too thinly, and cut out a 2.5cm (1in) circle for the hat brim. Take one flat head of the same, roll to a short sausage for the top of the hat and pinch out both ends.

38 Attach a strip of brown flower paste for the hat band. Trim to size.

39 Dampen the top of the hat and press it on the brim. Curl the top over.

40 Hollow out the middle of the hat with a ball tool so that it will fit on the head, and place it as shown.

41 Make a bow from brown flower paste strips as for the Fairy Dressing Up on page 75. Dampen and place on the back of the hat.

43 To make the goggles, roll black flower paste into two tiny balls, flatten them a little and use an 0.5cm (¼in) circle cutter to indent the middle.

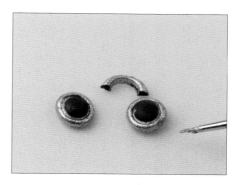

44 To make the nose piece, cut out a 0.5cm (¼in) ring and cut it in half. Paint the goggles with gold liquid food paint on a size 0000 brush.

42 Make a white sticking paste from Mexican paste and water, mixed with a palette knife. Apply this to the wings and stick them on to the fairy.

45 Dampen the goggles and place them on the brim of the hat. Squeeze a little piping gel into the lenses to make them shine. Attach a tiny edible gold sugar pearl to the choker with a small dot of piping gel.

46 You can make lots of additional steampunk style details for this fairy. For the shafts of the keys, make thin strands of Mexican paste 1.5cm (⅝in) long. Roll out Mexican paste thinly, cut out a 0.5cm (¼in) square and cut the teeth of the keys. For the key tops, cut a 0.5cm (¼in) circle and a 1cm (⅜in) oval. Mark small holes using a cocktail stick and join all the key pieces using water. For the hoops of the chain, cut out a 0.5cm (¼in) circle, flatten it slightly to make it larger, then cut it again. For the watch, repeat step 44, but with white Mexican paste. Make a hole in the top of the rim, which creates the watch case. Paint the keys, chain and watch case with gold liquid paint. Paint gold hands on the watch face. Attach the details using piping gel: the watch goes in the fairy's hand and the keys hang from their loop at her waist (see page 114).

This page and opposite
Details of the Steampunk Fairy.

Peacock Fairy

Carnival time brings out flamboyant fairies. This design was inspired by wonderful carnival costumes, and the trailing peacock feathers are perfect to adorn this gorgeous fairy. Tiny edible silver pearls frame the pretty headdress and the fairy sits in the crook of a tree stump to display the full length of her costume.

You will need

Mexican paste in chestnut, brown
Fairy head mould
Kebab/cake pop stick
Ball tool
Edible pen in coffee, black, blue, white, green
Edible powder food colour in pearl white, soft pink, turquoise, purple, pearl Pacific blue, dark brown, pearl crushed pine, deep purple
Pure food-grade alcohol
Size 0000 paintbrush
Black sugarpaste
Dresden tool
Flower paste in white, purple
Rolling pin
2.5cm (1in) circle cutter
1.25cm (½in) heart plunger cutter
Confectioner's dusting brush
Paper tissue
Petal veining tool
Tiny piping bag
Clear piping gel
Cocktail sticks
Tiny edible silver pearls
Palette knife
Water brushpen
4cm (1½in) heart cutter
Frill cutter
Cutting wheel
4cm (1½in) leaf/petal cutter
1cm (³/₈in) oval cutter
1cm (³/₈in) leaf/petal cutter
Tiny blossom plunger cutter
Edible wafer paper butterfly
Fine pointed scissors

1 Use the largest of the four fairy heads to make the head using chestnut Mexican paste, then make the body with four flat heads of the same paste rolled into an oval and then a peanut shape. Flatten the body slightly. Make arm sockets with the ball tool. Draw eyebrows with coffee edible pen, use black for the pupils and eyelashes, blue for the irises and pearl white edible powder food colour mixed with pure food-grade alcohol for the whites of the eyes and highlights, using a size 0000 paintbrush. Dust the cheeks with turquoise edible powder food colour on a confectioner's dusting brush. Paint the lips with soft pink edible powder food colour mixed in the same way.

2 Make hair from black sugarpaste as shown on page 15.

3 Knead turquoise edible powder food colour into white flower paste and roll it thinly. Allow to dry a little. Cut out a 2.5cm (1in) circle. Cut out a heart towards the bottom with a 1.25cm (½in) heart plunger cutter.

4 Use a confectioner's dusting brush to dust with purple edible powder food colour on the inside and outside edges.

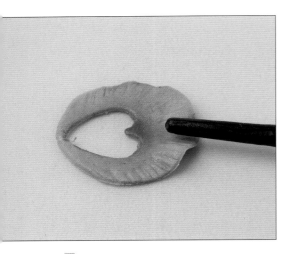

5 Dust on pearl Pacific blue edible powder food colour and then frill the edge with a petal veining tool to complete the headdress.

6 Dampen the hair. Cut the headdress at the bottom of the heart and press it on the head.

7 Use a tiny piping bag to pipe clear piping gel on the edges of the headdress. Dip the end of a cocktail stick in piping gel and pick up tiny silver balls to decorate the edge.

8 Roll brown Mexican paste to a very large sausage shape to make the tree trunk. Shape the top into a seat for the fairy and texture with a palette knife and a Dresden tool.

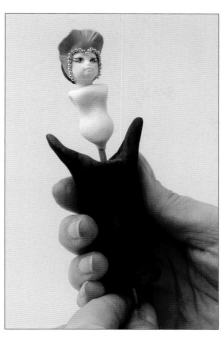

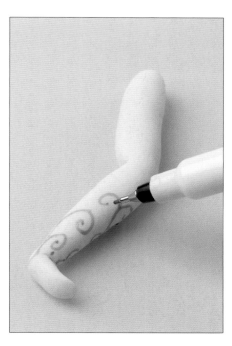

9 Dust the tree trunk with dark brown edible powder food colour.

10 Push the tree trunk on the stick below the fairy's body, leaving a little room for her legs.

11 Make each leg from two flat heads of chestnut Mexican paste. Draw on swirls in green edible pen.

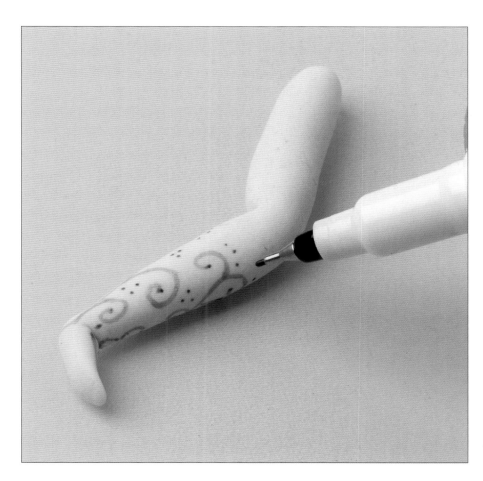

12 Add dots in blue edible pen.

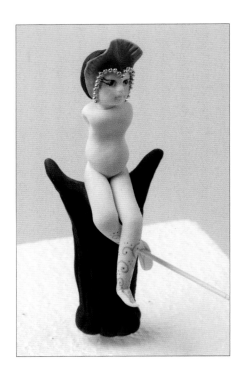

13 Push the fairy and tree trunk into a polystyrene block or something similar. Brush the base of the body with water and push on the legs. Add a cocktail stick to support the bent leg while it dries.

14 Roll out Mexican paste coloured with turquoise edible powder food colour and cut out a 4cm (1½in) heart. Dust round the edges with purple edible powder food colour, dampen the back and press on to the fairy for a bodice.

15 Roll out purple Mexican paste and cut to 7cm (2¾in) wide and around 15cm (5⅝in) long. Measure from the fairy's waist down to the base and a little more to get the length right for a swathe of fabric. Place one end over a frill cutter and use a rolling pin to create a clean edge.

16 Gather the non-frilled end of the piece, roll it flat and trim it with a cutting wheel, then dampen and attach to the back of the fairy. Curl it round to the front of the base.

17 To make the peacock feathers, roll out the turquoise-coloured Mexican paste, cut with a 4cm (1½in) leaf/petal cutter, indent down the centre with the Dresden tool and texture the edges at an angle with the petal veining tool.

18 Roll out purple flower paste, cut a 1cm (³/₈in) oval and place it on the feather for the eye.

19 Dust pearl crushed pine edible powder food colour on the feather.

20 Mix turquoise edible powder food colour with pure food-grade alcohol and paint an oval towards the top of the purple oval using a size 0000 paintbrush.

21 To complete the feather, paint deep purple edible powder food colour mixed with pure food-grade alcohol in the centre of the eye.

22 Make eighteen to twenty feathers. Curl them, dampen the backs and begin to place them at the bottom of the purple train.

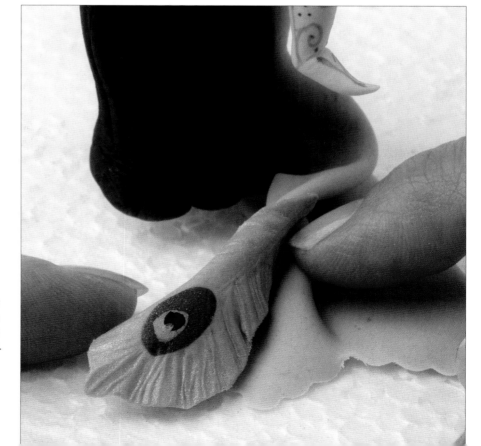

23 Continue building up the train until it is covered with peacock feathers. Add two feathers at the fairy's sides.

24 Roll out purple flower paste and cut twenty-six feathers with a 1cm (³/₈in) leaf/petal cutter. Dust one end of each with pearl Pacific edible powder food colour.

25 Frill the wide ends of the purple feathers with the petal veining tool. Dampen the bottom of the bodice and layer the feathers with the frilled ends downwards.

26 Make arms from one flat head each of chestnut Mexican paste, as on page 14. Dampen the arm sockets and attach the arms with one hand on the tree trunk as shown.

27 Dampen the shoulders and place three of the purple feathers on each.

28 Make more, longer hair from black sugarpaste and create a pony tail trailing down.

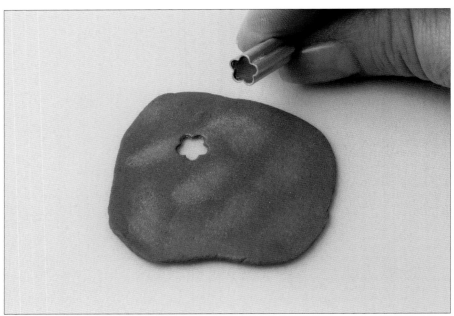

29 Roll out purple flower paste and dust it randomly with pearl Pacific blue edible powder food colour. Cut out five or six little flowers with a tiny blossom plunger cutter.

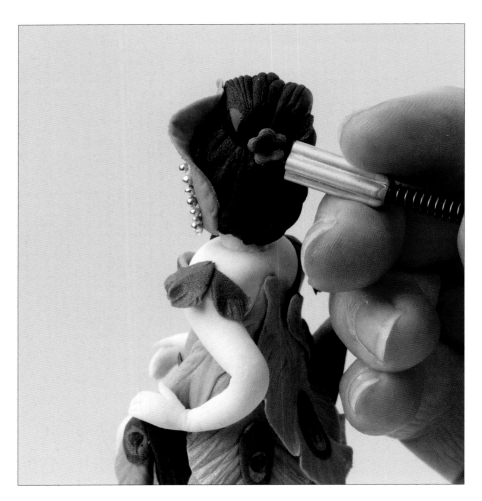

30 Dampen around the pony tail and use the plunger to push the flowers on.

31 Decorate round the pony tail up to the headdress.

32 Cut out a ready-made edible wafer paper butterfly for the wings using fine pointed scissors.

33 To finish the fairy, apply piping gel to the right side of the butterfly, bend it in the middle a little and stick it to her back. You may need to push in a pin while it dries.

This page and opposite
Details from the Peacock Fairy.

Index